BATTLING
THE OCEANS
IN A ROWBOAT

BATTLING
THE OCEANS
IN A ROWBOAT

CROSSING THE ATLANTIC AND

NORTH PACIFIC ON OARS AND GRIT

MICK DAWSON

CENTER
STREET®

NEW YORK   NASHVILLE

Center Street
Hachette Book Group
1290 Avenue of the Americas, New York, NY 10104
centerstreet.com
twitter.com/centerstreet

First Edition: August 2017

Center Street is a division of Hachette Book Group, Inc. The Center Street name
and logo are trademarks of Hachette Book Group, Inc.

The publisher is not responsible for websites (or their content)
that are not owned by the publisher.

The Hachette Speakers Bureau provides a wide range of authors for speaking events.
To find out more, go to www.HachetteSpeakersBureau.com or call (866) 376-6591.

Print book interior design by Timothy Shaner, NightandDayDesign.biz

Library of Congress Cataloging-in-Publication Data has been applied for.

ISBNs: 978-1-4789-4751-6 (hardcover), 978-1-4789-4752-3 (ebook)

Printed in the United States of America

LSC-C

10   9   8   7   6   5   4   3   2   1

This book is dedicated to my parents.

Little if anything contained in these pages

would have been possible without their

constant love, support, and example.

CONTENTS

CONTENTS

CONTENTS

BATTLING
THE OCEANS
IN A ROWBOAT

ROWING FOR MY LIFE

IN 1999, I was a former British Royal Marine struggling to find his way in life after leaving the service. Increasingly disillusioned and isolated, I knew I was looking for something, but I had no idea what.

Then I found my purpose. By 2001, I'd successfully rowed across the Atlantic Ocean and was determined to become the first person to row across the North Pacific from Japan to San Francisco.

Nearly a decade later, together with my friend and rowing partner Chris Martin, I accomplished that goal. This is the story of two successful Atlantic crossings, two less successful solo North Pacific crossings, and one glorious world first.

It's a story of ocean adventures where I would discover more about myself than I ever could have imagined. I hope I can do the people who helped make them possible justice in the pages that follow, particularly the three people who rowed with me. I went to sea with one brother and came back with three.

ALONE AT SEA

AUGUST 22, 2004. That morning, I was having the time of my life. By the end of the day, I was fighting to save it.

I'd been at sea, alone, unsupported, and without regular communications for 109 days in a rowing boat. Just to clarify, this was not the familiar type of rowboat that might be used on a lake or pond. This was a specially designed, totally self-sufficient ocean rowing boat. It was twenty-one and a half feet long and six feet across at its broadest point. A sealed bow section and a cabin at the back where I could sleep and shelter from the big storms sandwiched an open rowing deck in the middle. On the rowing deck there was the same sliding-seat assembly you'd find on a flat-water rowing boat, toughened up considerably to cope with the demands of an extended ocean rowing passage. I had rowed more than four and a half thousand miles across the North Pacific in that boat, departing Japan early in May. My goal was to become the first person to row across the North Pacific, finishing beneath the span of the Golden Gate Bridge in San Francisco.

That morning, with little more than fourteen hundred nautical miles between me and the finish line, I allowed myself to believe that success was within my grasp. But not for the first time, nor for the last, the North Pacific had other ideas.

Although it was the most challenging of my ocean rowing adventures, the North Pacific wasn't the first of them. That had been three years earlier, in 2001, with a three-thousand-mile voyage across the Atlantic with my brother, Steve.

We were both former Royal Marine commandos (the Royal Navy's elite amphibious soldiers), and both of us were desperate for a challenge. Rowing the Atlantic seemed to fit the bill. We built a boat, learned the basics of rowing, and along with another thirty-one boats pushed off from Tenerife in the Canary Islands in a race to Barbados. We arrived seventy days later.

It was a life-changing experience for the pair of us and a pivotal one for me. I thirsted for ever greater challenges. Few people had successfully rowed any ocean at that time, but none had successfully rowed from Japan to San Francisco.

I wanted to be the first.

Two years later, in April 2003, I put together a solo challenge to the North Pacific route. It came to grief less than a thousand miles off the coast of Japan. Dreadful weather had forced a delayed departure that had put me directly into the path of three major storms. The third had left my boat crippled with a smashed rudder. With no prospect of reaching North America, let alone San Francisco, I returned to Japan. My introduction to the brutal realities of the North Pacific was over.

As harsh as that introduction had been, though, there was nothing that persuaded me that my goal was impossible. My boat would have to be refitted to cope better with the severe conditions of the North Pacific. I would have to make sure I escaped the Japanese coast earlier in the spring. But I knew it could be done. My return to Japan the following year and my subsequent rapid progress toward San Francisco had justified that belief.

But now that progress was about to come to a halt.

The previous two days, I had been rowing in mountainous seas. As I would learn much later—but suspected at the time—two massive storm systems had collided a couple of hundred miles to the south of me. That collision in the middle of such a vast ocean had in turn created an enormous swell, which radiated out from the epicenter of the battling storm systems for hundreds of miles in every direction, like angry ripples racing away from two huge rocks dropped into the center of a pond.

The ocean around me became a watery version of the rolling countryside of the Sussex downs on the south coast of England, which was now my home. But this was a vast, roaring and much wetter version.

Though it is awe-inspiring to view from the deck of a twenty-one-foot boat, a huge rolling ocean isn't necessarily a threat to such a vessel. I'd rowed through similar conditions before as I'd skirted typhoons, and I'd learned how to cope with them. Once I'd come to terms with the intimidating scale of these seas, I had developed and mastered a technique that kept me safe while still allowing me to make forward progress. The added problem on this occasion was that because of the relatively close proximity of the two storm systems, I was also being hit by large, flat breaking waves. Those waves were almost independent of the huge swells roaring toward me.

Large breaking waves capsize small boats, especially small rowboats. To make matters worse, the waves were coming at me from a chaotic variety of directions. In sailing terms it's what's known as a confused sea, but this was "confused" on an epic scale. Still, there was a discernible trend in the direction of the swell toward the east, where I was headed.

Whenever it was feasible to make headway toward the east, I rowed relentlessly, regardless of conditions and despite rain and wind, protected only by my knowledge and experience. Despite the challenging weather, I stayed on the oars. For forty-eight hours I battled my way toward the US coast on the back of this thunderous, unpredictable, and terrifying maritime roller coaster. I gritted my teeth and pushed my fears of the hostile environment to the back of my mind. A stubborn determination to gain every mile to the east was my only focus.

I set the boat and myself up to deal with the daunting yet undeniably exhilarating conditions as safely and efficiently as possible. Safely is, of course, a relative term when you are talking about a small plywood boat in a near hurricane.

I would watch the colossal mountains of water rearing up behind my tiny boat, carrying on their backs rows of deadly breaking waves twenty to thirty feet high that tumbled down toward me one behind the other. The noise was as terrifying as the sight, a thunderous roar, as if heaven and earth were competing to see which of them could shout the loudest. Water crashed into the aft of my boat, smashing over her and me at times, passing beneath us at others, occasionally lifting us up on a surf-edged magic carpet ride of speed. It would be an adrenaline-fueled couple of days.

Even as the boat and I were pummeled by waves and battered for hours on end, an almost unbearable drain on energy and morale, I kept going by doing what generations of sailors, and for that matter Royal Marines, have done: I concentrated on what was in front of me, the small but crucial tasks, taking my mind, if not my body, out of the storm.

I stowed everything on board securely, attached the safety leash that connected me to the boat around my ankle, and ballasted the vessel with gallons of seawater in heavy-duty black trash can liners, tying a simple knot in the top to secure the water inside. I stowed them along the keel of my boat in the center lockers, where they'd be most effective in helping to keep the boat upright. I moved my rowing position further back to gain as much protection as possible from the aft cabin.

In everything I did, I kept the weight of the boat low and central, with a bias toward the back to make her additionally resistant to broaching (going side on to the sea) and capsizing. In particular, the threat was from the sideswiping rogue waves that were broadsiding me on a regular basis in the confused sea.

I strung out a long line with a small drogue on the end. A drogue is a small canvas version of the much larger nylon para anchor I carried on board. It was designed only to slow the boat's progress, not halt it completely like the para anchor. I deployed it from the stern. It created a predisposition for the boat to run with the stern toward the prevailing waves. That reduced my rowing speed a little but didn't halt it. Above all, it meant that despite the huge waves crashing over the back of the boat, submerging it and me at times, the vessel remained upright, relatively stable, and pointing in the right direction.

Even when racing in the surf at the top of the occasional passing wave I was able to harness, my boat, *Mrs D*, named in honor of my long-suffering mother, Mrs. Dawson, remained, much like her namesake, defiantly rock solid. That allowed me to keep heading east toward that beautiful California bridge as swiftly and safely as possible despite the dreadful conditions.

One of the things that kept me going, as it does for many long-distance sailors and rowers, was music. Music can play an extraordinarily powerful part in an ocean row. With the around-the-clock rowing schedule, it's your only constant companion apart from the ocean. With nothing to distract you hour after hour, you find new meaning and emotion even in songs you've heard a thousand times before.

My brother and Atlantic rowing partner, Steve, had a much more in-depth and eclectic knowledge of music than I had, so when I had been preparing for this row, I'd asked him if he'd create a playlist for me. I wanted not just the standard stuff I'd chosen but other music I might not normally find time for. I'd never have a better opportunity to discover it.

Steve's musical playlist took on increasingly greater significance once I lost communication on day 12. I listened over and over to the Beautiful South, with their layered lyrics and addictive melodies, the blues greats, even pop songs from my youth. They were my only connection with home and normal life. The emotional impact of some of the songs was enormously powerful. I seriously doubt that there's a better place in the world to listen too and appreciate Louis Armstrong's classic "What a Wonderful World" than from the deck of an ocean rowing boat, particularly beneath a full moon on a cloudless, star-filled night. The power possessed in the song's incredible lyrics was magnified beyond belief as I fought my solitary war of attrition against the Pacific.

Whereas the Atlantic route is based on the usually light trade winds blowing steadily toward the Caribbean, the North Pacific crossing from Japan to the United States offers no such assistance. The winds and currents conspire constantly to prevent or slow any east heading. Every mile gained on the North Pacific is vulnerable to the next weather front or rogue stretch of current snatching it back. There was a reason nobody had ever successfully rowed from Japan to the Golden Gate Bridge.

As weeks turned into months, the mental challenge of fighting through the constant battles was taking their toll. Alone with my thoughts as a result of the satellite phone breaking in a storm, I only had the music from the deck speakers and a camera to record my adventures to distract me. I rowed for as many hours a day as possible, sometimes up to eighteen. I ached all over, and the constant chafe on my body was painfully uncomfortable. All that, combined with the seemingly endless loss of miles, was mental torture.

I found myself screaming out in frustration at the constant and seemingly unwinnable battle with the conditions. Ludicrously, and in typically British fashion, when I did so, I remember always looking behind me first in case anyone could see me making a fool of myself.

I was exhausted physically and mentally, rowing every possible hour I could to make progress against my relentless foe. Then, at a point when I felt I was at the bottom of an emotional well, drowning in self-pity, a song from Steve's playlist came on. I'd never heard it before, but it transformed my mood and mental state beyond all recognition. I was as near to feeling defeated as I'd ever come when out of the deck speakers floated the words of a song comparing life to being on a raging sea in a rowboat—exactly as I was. Fighting a constant battle against the waves that are trying to stop you achieving your goal—as I was. But most crucial of all were the final two lines of the verse:

Never, never, never, never, never give up
Those waves will see you safely to a friendly shore.

It was the last two lines to a verse in a Divine Comedy song called "Charmed Life." It is a wonderfully uplifting melodic homage to songwriter Neil Hannon's baby daughter. The whole song had resonance for me, as I'd always considered I'd lived a charmed life. The impact of that verse, though, shook me. It was as if somebody had whispered those words into my ear:

Never, never, never, never, never give up
Those waves will see you safely to a friendly shore.

Those words seemed to me to have been created specifically to drag me through that moment of despair. My morale and my strength were miraculously renewed, I would never, never, never, never, never give up, and those waves *would* see me to a friendly shore.

EARLY ON

CHALLENGES, particularly difficult ones, have been an essential requirement in my life from an early age. Arguably the toughest of them all came just a few weeks after my sixteenth birthday.

That was when I chose to swap the playing fields and classrooms of my hometown secondary school in Boston, nestling in the sleepy, flat county of Lincolnshire, for the assault courses and speed marches of Royal Marine commando training in the lung-busting hills of Devon.

As far back as I can remember, my only dream was to go to sea. That dream naturally evolved into an ambition to join the Royal Navy, before fate stepped in almost at the last minute and I chose a slightly different path, joining the Royal Marines, the navy's elite commando fighting force. Looking back on my childhood growing up in Boston, it's easy now to see how that ambition took root and how my future was shaped.

My parents, Derek and Joyce Dawson, both Boston-born and -bred, were ambitious and hardworking publicans, the youngest in the town at only twenty-three and twenty, respectively, when they took possession of their first pub, the Magnet Tavern. Remarkably and very proudly, five decades later they would also go on to become the town's oldest publicans.

Over the years they ran a total of three pubs in Boston before finally buying a country pub, the Cowbridge House Inn, on the outskirts of town. It was the only pub in England with that name, as my dad would proudly inform everyone, given the opportunity.

The second of the pubs we lived in was called the Woad Man, as in the blue battle paint made famous by Mel Gibson in the movie *Braveheart*. The Woad Man was a thriving business, a traditional local pub at a time when pubs were both numerous and the social hubs of their communities. It was an incredibly demanding and full-time occupation for both of my parents, and making it a success while at the same time raising a young family totally consumed them. They loved it, though, and in very different ways both were born publicans.

When we moved into the Woad Man, I was five and about to begin my first year at school. The relocation to the other side of town meant I would have to attend a different school from that of my older and only sibling, Steve.

Rather than have us attend different schools however, my grandmother on my mother's side, Nan, as we called her, offered a solution: she would collect us both each morning and take the pair of us to her and my grandfather's house, which was just around the corner from the school that Steve already attended, enabling both of us to go to the same one.

It also meant lots of early-morning four-mile-long walks through Boston that remain some of my most vivid and in many ways fondest childhood memories. They're certainly among the most significant.

Boston is a small port town on the east coast of England. About eighty miles north of London as the crow flies, it was founded on the banks of a tidal river called the Haven. The river gave the town access to the sea and provided a route for the commerce and trade that would provide the town's initial prosperity.

A busy if small commercial dock thrived during my childhood, along with a healthy inshore fishing fleet. Indications of Boston's original wealth, created largely from exports of wool in the 1300s and 1400s, when it was second only to London in the nation as a port, were evident in several of the grander constructions along the riverbanks, none more so than the spectacular and imposing form of its most famous landmark, St. Botolph's Church. It is a parish church as striking as many cathedrals, possessing a single tower some 272 feet high, the tallest church tower in England without a spire, which gives the church its ungodly nickname, "Boston Stump."

We would often walk directly by the Stump along the cobbled and atmospheric old roads that surrounded it, but whichever route we took we would find ourselves in its shadow, as the church dominates not only the riverbank and town center where it stands but also much of the surrounding countryside.

Decades later, my brother Steve and I, having successfully rowed across the Atlantic together, were invited to climb to the top of the Stump and stand at the very pinnacle of its famous tower. The public are allowed up to the second balcony, about two-thirds of the way up, but to stand on the top level was a rare privilege and a genuine honor. It was certainly something we could never in our wildest dreams have imagined doing as we wandered by as children on those early-morning outings.

Depending on the route we took across town, we'd cross the Haven, which neatly bisected the town, on one of two bridges. At the modern Haven Bridge we'd pass the river at its widest point, where the fishing fleet would be rafted up three deep when in port. The boats and the men who worked there were a tantalizing glimpse to a five-year-old of the exciting and dangerous life that existed just out of sight, where the sea and all its adventures beckoned. That river, particularly the broad stretch where the fishing boats tied up, was like an ocean to me, the widest and scariest stretch of water I'd ever seen.

The Haven carved its way through the center of town. Sometimes at low water it was little more than a meandering stream running between two huge glistening mud banks, while at high tide it became a seemingly unstoppable conveyor belt of heaving water threatening and sometimes breaching the flood walls placed at the top of the banks to contain it. It was always a mesmerizing sight to me.

The Grand Sluice Bridge, known locally as the Sluice, was our alternative and more regular route across the Haven. Built, as the name suggests, to house sluice gates and locks to control the flow of water, it marked the end of the saltwater Haven's progress inland and the start of the freshwater River Witham. There was a narrow single lane of traffic each way and a pedestrian footpath on either side of the old and ornate bridge. Old-fashioned ironwork formed the railings along the footpath on either side. The bridge sat upon huge stone pillars that supported it and formed the locks beneath. A railway box and gates sat at one end of the bridge, with huge iron arched supports heading off at an angle forming a separate but equally imposing railway bridge. At five years of age it seemed to me like an engineering marvel.

The Sluice Bridge also held the wonderful promise that if we were lucky the lock gates might be open as we crossed and we could look down on vast torrents of roaring white water disgorging from the Witham into the Haven just beneath our feet. That was wonderfully exciting and gave a thrilling demonstration of the enormous power of the river.

Both bridges provided a feast for the ravenous imagination of an impressionable young boy, and whichever one we crossed it was the highlight of those long dawn walks across town.

In reality they were nothing more than two unremarkable

bridges crossing an unremarkable river in a quiet and unremarkable Lincolnshire town. To my young and developing imagination, however, they were so much more than that; they were my first introduction to the excitement of the sea and its magnetic and hypnotic appeal. Even at such a young age I recognized that appeal, and I welcomed it, but I had no idea how that appeal would come to dominate and define my life.

If the seeds of my future maritime life were sown on those dawn walks across town, they were most definitely watered and fed at my grandparents' house.

My great-grandmother, who lived with my grandparents, was approaching her nineties when I was beginning school. She was the daughter of Irish immigrants, gypsies who'd gone to London in the late 1800s. She'd grown up in Whitechapel when Jack the Ripper was carving his dark legend on the same streets where she played as a girl. I remember her scaring Steve and me with stories of "Jack." She called him that almost as if she knew him, which only added to the thrill, and how she'd known the Flower Girls, as she called his victims, and the places where they were murdered. She was a formidable lady even in old age, and those Gothic stories only served to enhance that impression.

Gran's sister would eventually emigrate to Canada, and her two brothers both joined the Royal Navy as young men. That was the beginning of my family's connection with that great institution, sadly one that began on a desperately tragic note. In the early stages of World War I, my gran received a telegram from the king. Both of her brothers, whom she'd brought up as sons, had been killed in action on the same day. Gran had long white hair always tied neatly in a bun when I knew her as an old lady decades later. Apparently it had turned white overnight when she received that news.

My family could probably have been forgiven for having little if any time for the Royal Navy after that dreadful event. However, anyone walking into my grandparents' home, as Steve and I did each school day morning, would have seen immediately that that was far from the case.

As you walked through the front door, to the right was the front room, or parlor. The largest room in the house, it was always immaculate and contained pretty much everything of value my grandparents possessed. A piano that nobody ever played stood next to a settee and chairs that nobody ever sat on in front of a fireplace that nobody ever lit.

At the heart of the room, on the center of the dark polished wooden sideboard next to the silent piano, was a large black-and-white framed picture of a young man with matinee-idol good looks smiling broadly, resplendent in his Royal Navy Warrant Officer's No. 1 uniform and cap.

That was a picture of my mum's brother, my uncle Peter. He'd joined the Royal Navy right out of school and in doing so had banished the legacy of grief and loss that connected my family to the Royal Navy and replaced it with an enormous sense of pride. He was on display at the center of the room because he was the center of my grandparents' world. Not only had he gone on to bigger and better things outside of Boston, he'd also laid the ghosts of those two lost brothers to rest. The story of the Royal Navy and my family no longer ended with their tragic loss; my uncle had now effectively continued that story and in doing so had given meaning to that loss.

Once inside my grandparents' home, seeing that picture as the focal point of their most cherished room, the message was clear: if you wanted to be admired and respected in my family, you joined the Royal Navy.

As long as I can remember, my ambition, fueled by all the time I spent at my grandparents', had been to join the Royal Navy and go to sea. Although the marines are very much part of the Royal

Navy, joining them was a considerable departure from that goal. My brother, Steve, gets the credit for that change of direction.

As I entered my last year at school, Steve decided to join the marines and was going through the long and highly selective application process required for acceptance for training. Everything about that process—as it's designed to be—was exciting and increasingly enticing to an impressionable fifteen-year-old such as myself. So much so that ultimately I decided to follow in my brother's footsteps and enlist.

Within weeks of blowing out the sixteen candles on that year's birthday cake, I found myself embarking on what is regarded as the hardest basic military training in the world. It would certainly feel that way to me.

Although tougher challenges would follow, Royal Marine commando training remains to me the most difficult challenge I have ever undertaken. After that training I would never again, no matter how daunting the task, be as unprepared for what I had to face. I would also never again encounter such a steep and unforgiving learning curve. Training was a nine-month trial that would ultimately turn me from a snot-nosed schoolboy into a Royal Marine commando.

Be it brainwashing or conditioning—depending on whether you consider the process a bad or good thing—Royal Marine training works. It has to work because it needs to produce young men who when required can deal with the most unimaginable and terrifying situations and deal with them instinctively and with a calm professionalism. In the 1980s, Royal Marine training was a meat grinder, a highly effective one, that produced the required product at the end.

On August 3, 1980, sixty-three strangers and I stepped off a train together at Commando Training Centre Royal Marines Lympstone (better known as Lympstone Commando). A sixty-fifth guy didn't even get off the train. We had departed from every point in Great Britain, and the only thing we had in common as we stood on that arrival platform was our shared apprehension at what was to come.

Together we would form 268 Troop. None of us was older than seventeen. We were the latest batch of meat to be fed into the grinder. Nine tough months later, fewer than a third of us would emerge as fully fledged Royal Marines.

Initially I adapted well to training. With the advantage of a brother who'd recently finished the course, I knew to a large extent what to expect. Many of my colleagues had no idea; they tended to be the ones who left first. I was fit and reasonably capable, and despite the hardships, I mostly enjoyed the experience.

As training progressed and intensified, the mental and physical pressures increased for all of us. Commando training is meant to be many things, but one thing it's not meant to be is easy. Alarmingly for me, and adding to that pressure, I began to develop increasingly painful knee problems. After any kind of major physical exercise, of which there's a lot in Royal Marine training, both my knees would swell and hurt like hell.

I took copious amounts of painkillers and hoped for the best, but the condition continued to plague me as the weeks passed and the workload increased. The last thing I wanted to do was go to sick bay but eventually I had to, if only to get some more effective painkillers. The doctor took one look at my knees, wrote me a prescription for anti-inflammatory pills, and painkillers and said, 'No phiz for two weeks and no boots.'

To my mind it was a death sentence for my ambitions to become a Royal Marine. It's probably a good indication of my age and emotional maturity (or lack there of), that I remember almost bursting into tears as he said that.

"No phiz" is Royal Marine shorthand for "no physical training." The troop had major tests to complete in just a few days. If I didn't pass those, tests I wouldn't progress any further with 268 Troop. There were no exceptions; you made the grade, or you were out. In the ruthless and unforgiving process, I would be "back-trooped."

Being back-trooped meant being taken out of the troop you had joined with and, after a rehab period to recover from your injury, being placed in a troop coming through behind, joining the new troop at pretty much the same point where you had left your old one. Everybody was terrified of the prospect of being back-trooped, and I was no exception. At best, you end up being an outsider in the new troop you join; at worst, you're hated and seen as a weak link.

My only emotional anchor in the harsh environment that was Royal Marines training had become the strangers I'd stepped off the train with on August 3—at least those who still remained by that stage. In the pressure-cooker environment of our training, I had already formed close friendships that have lasted to this day, almost four decades later.

Even beyond the tight circle of close friends I'd made, the troop as a whole had become an extended and mutually supportive family. The familiar faces and the shared experiences, particularly the hardships, gave us a bond that drew us together and created a strength greater than any individual. That, as I would discover, was a template for service life in general. The last thing I wanted to do was leave my new family and join a troop of strangers.

The doctor explained that it was purely the physical stresses being put on my young and still growing body that were causing the problems. Carrying heavy weights on your back over miles of rough ground and running in boots wearing full kit, occasionally with a bloke and his full kit on your back, can have that effect. "You won't need surgery. Rest will sort it out," he assured me—rest, of course, being the rarest and most valuable of commodities in Royal Marine training.

I stood up to leave his office in a state of shock. In my hand was the pink "No phiz" chit he'd handed me.

"Give that to the MA [medical assistant] on your way out, and I'll see you in two weeks," he said.

I walked out of the office in a daze and looked across at the MA sitting at his desk. Without even thinking, I slipped the pink slip into my pocket and left the sick bay, nodding at the MA on the way out. I didn't even get the painkillers and anti-inflammatories I so desperately needed. I'd take my chances with my knees breaking down; It was a better option than the certainty of being back-trooped.

During the examination, I'd mentioned to the doctor that we had tests coming up that I couldn't afford to miss as they were the gateway to the second half of training. His answer had been dismissive: "You'll never pass anything with knees in that condition, Dawson."

That pronouncement hung around my neck like a slowly tightening noose for the remainder of training. In many ways it became as debilitating psychologically as the actual physical problems with my knees. My confidence was shattered, and I expected my suspect knees to fail me at any moment from then on. For the first time I thought I wasn't going to make it. I lost belief in myself. Training was already difficult; for me, from that point on, it became considerably more so.

However, as everything in my fresh young world seemed to be crumbling around me, it turned out that I had one saving grace, which up to that point I'd been completely unaware of. I was stubborn.

At the end of marine training we would take our final commando tests, after which, should we pass them, we would receive our coveted green berets and become fully fledged Royal Marines. Always my own harshest critic and very much laboring under the problems with my knees, I felt I was just scraping through as we approached the final test.

The commando tests are an exhausting series of various assault courses, grueling military obstacle courses, and speed marches complete with equipment and weapons and with set time limits. They're run on consecutive days, so there's little time for recovery. The process is exhausting both mentally and physically. The final test is the 30-miler. It's a "yomp," or march across rough ground, with full fighting gear and weapons, over a 30-mile course, to be completed within eight hours. If the weather's good, it's relatively straightforward.

For our 30-miler, the weather was atrocious. Heavy rain and damp, heavy mist meant that Dartmoor, the setting of the Sherlock Holmes classic *The Hound of the Baskervilles*, was a navigational nightmare. With an eight-hour time limit, we found ourselves at the halfway mark, 15 miles, having already taken five hours. It looked very much as if the whole troop were going to fail, which would be a disaster.

The one thing in our favor was that the last fifteen miles were largely along roads and paths, so the ground underfoot was less like the bog we'd dragged ourselves through to that point.

The troop officer, who was probably already worrying about how he was going to explain a 100 percent fail rate, gathered together a small group of guys he thought might make the tight cutoff time (I was not one of them) and set off. The rest of us were told to run as fast as we could.

For me those last fifteen miles seemed like Napoleon's retreat from Moscow. Guys were dropping out or dropping back all along the route. Everybody was desperate to make the finish line inside the remaining three hours. Everybody was worn out, not just by the weeks of exertion but also by the pressure of nine months of intense training all hanging on this frantic run for home.

I set off alongside my friend Ross Cluett. He would go on to have a long and distinguished career in the marines. Together Ross and I somehow caught up to the troop officer and the group he'd initially set off with, or at least what remained of them. I'm not sure who was more surprised, him or us. With the cutoff time looming, the last few hundred meters were a sprint to the finish. Ross and I were among the first in, with just a couple of minutes to spare.

My performance with Ross on that 30-miler, at least the last 15 miles of it, convinced me that I was worthy of my place in the Royal Marines. I felt I had finally demonstrated the qualities worthy of the corps I was joining. Whatever my shortcomings, I possessed a stubborn determination to finish whatever I started. It was a characteristic I would come to depend heavily on in my ocean rowing adventures.

DISASTER STRIKES

THROUGHOUT MY SOLO VOYAGE from Japan to California, I tried to film every aspect of the row. One of my principal aims was to capture, and on my return show, the conditions on board a very small rowboat traversing the little-explored waters of the North Pacific.

That two-day battle with the ocean at its worst, despite the challenging conditions, was a cinematic opportunity I couldn't miss. Fixed cameras and regular battery changes allowed me to capture every moment, including some of the most thrilling and exciting rowing footage of the whole voyage. It was only when the storm had finally passed on that August 22 morning, when my boat and I had emerged relatively unscathed from the fight, that disaster struck while I was preparing to film the nearly flat calm following the storm.

The dark clouds and roaring waves of the previous two days had been replaced by oppressively gray, overcast skies and a sea drained of its previous furious energy. The huge roaring walls of water tumbling down mountainous seas had now been reduced to an almost lazy rolling seascape. The visibility was poor, the wind almost non-existent, and heavy showers were frequent.

The effect of the heavy showers on the seemingly exhausted ocean was particularly dramatic. The rain's torrential impact completely flattened out what remained of the waves, while creating an eerie clinging mist just above sea level. I could see only a few dozen yards in any direction from my boat. But what I could see looked more like the steaming surface of some alien planet than the Pacific Ocean. The comparison to the previous two days could not have been starker. To capture that contrast, I retreated to "the Nest," my tiny cabin at the back of the boat, to prepare my video camera.

Inside the cabin I couldn't have been more content; the rain was hammering on the roof, making it even more pleasant to be inside. Despite the rain, the change in the weather had made life on board much more bearable. I was looking forward to the days ahead.

One moment I was sitting comfortably in the enclosed cabin at the back of the boat, camera in hand, listening to the beating rain on the roof. The next, the boat was being picked up by what seemed a celestial hand and rolled effortlessly onto her roof.

There was no impact as such, as a collision with a whale or a passing ship might have produced. To my mind, then as now, it was undoubtedly wave action that had rolled the boat. But where had such a wave come from in these flat calm conditions? How had this boat, which had just negotiated two days of monstrous seas and survived months of regular storm-force conditions, suddenly been capsized in a windless, flat ocean? Regardless of what the cause might be, she was going over and I was trapped inside, helpless.

I remember that my first thought was that she was being rolled in the bow wave of an unseen ship, and I braced myself for the inevitable impact. The whole of the voyage, I'd been plagued by constant and terrifying near misses with passing commercial ships. Four times I'd rowed from under the bows of those leviathans with only yards to spare, as they emerged unheralded at great speeds over the horizon.

In 2004, there were no electronic systems available that could reliably "paint" my plywood vessel's position onto the radar screen of a passing ship. Lookouts, even in the unlikely event that a ship employed them in the barren stretches of the Pacific, were unlikely to pick me up visually even if they knew I was there. I needed to spot the ships myself, and I needed to take action to avoid collision. A collision would have been catastrophic for me but go completely unnoticed by any ship.

On one occasion earlier in the voyage, I'd emerged from a week of rowing in dense fog only to look over my shoulder and see, just a few hundred yards away, a huge, strangely empty container ship steaming toward me. It was a Maersk vessel. I could identify that much by the beige superstructure and blue hull common to the line even before I saw the Maersk name emblazoned along her hull.

With the absence of containers on board (presumably she was heading to Asia for maintenance or refit), which would normally tower above the deck, her profile was much lower than normal and her beige superstructure merged into the mist. She was right on top of me before I saw her. I was alarmingly only a couple of hundred yards away and being blown directly into her path, although I judged not quickly enough to escape safely to the other side if I attempted to row across her bow. I was now in a bizarre situation where I was going to run into a ship as opposed to it running into me. I immediately threw a drogue over the side to help stop or at least slow my progress into the path of this unstoppable metallic monster, and I grabbed my VHF radio: "Unknown commercial vessel, this is ocean rowing boat *Mrs D*. I am one hundred meters off your port bow, and there is a risk of collision! I say again, unknown commercial vessel, this is ocean rowing boat *Mrs D*. I am off your port bow, and there's a risk of collision!"

The officer of the watch who responded sounded as though he'd fallen off his chair with shock as he breathlessly acknowledged my emergency message. To my horror he immediately began to turn his vessel hard to starboard (the right). Unfortunately for me, by that stage I was so close to the hull of the ship and the ship was so huge that it meant that the stern of the vessel, with its massive churning propeller, was going to swing round and smash into me.

"Unknown vessel, STOP!! Stop turning!" I cried into the radio. "You'll run me down with the back of the ship if you continue to turn!"

Thankfully the officer of the watch reacted again just as swiftly and stopped his abrupt emergency turn to starboard. I stood help-less on the deck of my rowing boat, holding my breath as one of the largest ships in the world passed within spitting distance. The churn-ing white waters produced by the propeller only yards away from me buffeted my tiny boat as the ship eventually, much to my relief, slipped safely by.

After the drama of our initial introduction, the officer of the watch and I settled down for a bit of a chat, albeit a faceless one con-ducted over the short-range VHF radio. I'd had no communication with land since early in my voyage, when my satellite phone had been damaged in a storm. Ironically, these all-too-regular terrifying near misses actually provided a welcome contact with other human beings for me. I told him my name and asked if he could relay a mes-sage home to let everyone know I was okay and, despite the broken sat phone, doing well. As with all such messages, I hoped the circum-stances of our meeting would not come up when relayed. I felt that my family probably had enough to worry about at that stage without sharing the crippling fear of collision and its consequences that I'd developed.

The officer of the watch introduced himself as Paulios Henrik, or at least that's what it sounded like, from the Faeroe Islands. I've never forgotten his name. He said he'd be happy to contact my family for me and also asked if I would answer a question for him.

"Of course," I said. "What question?"

"Mick," he said, "what are you doing on a rowing boat in the middle of the Pacific Ocean?"

"Well," I replied, "I was out fishing . . ."

He was true to his word and did relay my message home (I'd later find out that he had done so without detailing the dramatic nature of our meeting), and he wished me well and a safe and successful onward journey. His last words to me, as his ship was disappearing over the horizon, were, "Mick. You English. You some crazy bastards!" I've been called worse.

In the chaos of my present predicament I wasn't anticipating such a pleasantly amusing conclusion. I was rolling around the cabin of my capsizing rowing boat, amid a sort of eerie, desolate quiet, and in my imagination just waiting for the huge steel bow of an unseen ship to come crashing through the bulkhead or, worse, to be dragged into its thrashing, devastating propeller blades. Those were terrifying moments and the embodiment of collision nightmares, which had haunted me throughout the voyage. But the impact never came, and if any churning propeller blades did pass by, they failed to draw me to my doom.

Yet I realized that my problems were just beginning. The agonizing roll of the boat continued. Trapped inside the cabin, I realized I'd failed to close the hatch securely behind me, and water was now gushing in around the seal as the cabin submerged. Despite the chaos and disorientation of the capsizing, I managed to grab hold of the handle and secure the watertight seal on the hatch, cutting off the deadly inrushing ocean, although not before a substantial amount of seawater had flooded in.

The momentum of the roll began to slow, partly as the energy of the freak wave that had caused the capsizing diminished and partly because the free-flowing water that had entered the cabin was working against the natural self-righting design of the boat.

Like a highly excited hamster in a sealed exercise wheel, I tried to use my body weight to help force the boat around and complete her 360-degree roll. But just at the point when any further movement would make the boat pop back upright, sickenly, slowly she ground to a halt.

For what must have been just the briefest of seconds but felt like an eternity to me, she hung suspended between salvation and disaster. Ten degrees further around, and she'd emerge upright, relatively unscathed. Ten degrees further back, and I was literally sunk. Finally, and with what I would swear was an audible groan from my beloved boat, she gave up the fight, rolled back onto her side, and lay motionless, crippled in the flat calm, foreboding waters of the North Pacific.

After the turmoil and panic of the capsize I now found myself in a strangely still and silent world. The boat had come to rest half submerged on her starboard side. The cabin was partially flooded, and gear and equipment were floating across the surface of the seawater that had rushed in through the unsealed hatch.

The only break in the silence was the unnatural, unnerving sound of water lapping around the inside of the cabin. I looked out through the half-submerged entrance hatch at an incongruous split-screen view of the world outside. The top half was the surface of an empty and relatively flat Pacific. The bottom half was that of the crystal clear waters beneath, complete with a school of fish looking curiously in at me. If the clock hadn't already been ticking on my survival from the minute I left Japan, it started ticking then.

SINKING FEELING

ONE OF THE REASONS for my attempt to row across the North Pacific in the first place was a desperate need for a challenge, a need I've had since childhood. Trapped in my crippled rowing boat more than a thousand miles from the US coast, I now faced the greatest challenge of my life.

My boat was just a fraction over twenty-one feet long and made from reinforced, epoxy-coated marine plywood. Fully provisioned and equipped at the start of the voyage, she weighed in at about a ton. At the rear, where I was now trapped, was the "watertight" cabin section. The bulkhead housing the main entry hatch was the broadest part of the cabin, at about five and a half feet. The cabin itself tapered to a width of less than eighteen inches at the transom, the very back of the boat.

When resting, I could stretch out to just about full length. On my previous two-man row across the Atlantic I had even managed to sleep, when storms hit, with my brother, Steve, crammed in beside me. The ability to sleep is a testament more to the exhaustion that constantly accompanies you on an ocean rowing boat than to any comfort afforded on board. Cooking and ablutions were very basic. A bucket stowed on deck provided the toilet and coined the ocean rowing phrase "Bucket and chuck it," the stock answer to the question "How do you go to the loo?"—always followed by "after checking the wind direction!" Cooking was done on a simple gas camping stove with replacement canisters—always outside, as gas fumes in the cabin could potentially be fatal. The majority of the food on board was dehydrated, boil in a bag, so it was simply a matter of boiling water. Some of the food was hydrated and ready to eat from its packing, so even if you couldn't cook on deck you could eat something, albeit cold, inside the cabin when the storms hit.

The cabin deck head, or roof, curved overhead like an angular igloo and slanted down toward the stern. It was just about high enough to sit upright in by the entry hatch, providing you assumed a kind of fetal position. In reality the cabin was little more than a sleeping capsule and a welcome refuge from severe weather when needed. Steve and I had christened it "the Nest" during our Atlantic adventure.

The electrical systems and controls were all fitted inside the cabin to provide the vulnerable electronics as much protection as possible from the elements, making it not only the bedroom but also the nerve center of the boat. Beneath the cabin floor, which was covered with thin, removable, waterproof mattress sections, was a series of lockers of varying sizes and capacities that stretched the full length of the boat in three rows, fourteen of them in total. That created a highly effective series of watertight bulkheads designed to prevent sinking while adding integral strength to the vessel. If the boat's stores are correctly stowed between these bulkheads with the majority of the weight low and along the center line of the boat, this would aid the boat's inherent ability to self-right.

The lockers in the floor of the cabin also housed the most precious and potentially fragile items on board, including my film equipment, the life-giving water-making unit and its motor, as well as the heartbeat of the boat, two 12-volt batteries similar to what you'd find in any car. Those were recharged daily by solar panels fitted to the outside of the boat.

A battery management system controlled the charging and discharging process and provided me with a constant readout of battery strength and performance. Practically every electronic item and system on board used those two main batteries as their primary source of power, from navigation and lighting to CD player and rechargeable VHF radios. That system and the power it provided were the lifeblood of the boat and the lifeblood of the row.

Forward of the cabin was a hatch that opened onto the rowing deck. It was slightly longer in length than the cabin but completely open, with no cover or roof. There was a large foot well immediately beneath the hatch that you could step down into (the only position on the boat where you could safely stand up) and two small bulwarks running along either side about twelve inches high, offering at least some protection from the sea.

Several self-sealing scuppers (flaps) were built into the bulwarks so that when the deck was flooded (as it frequently would be when waves crashed over the boat or during heavy rain), the water could easily roll off the deck. The width of the rowing deck was approximately five and a half feet across its length, which was slightly curved, forming the central element of the boat connecting the more sharply tapering bow and stern sections.

The other most noticeable features were the sliding-seat assembly that ran down the center of the deck and the adjustable footplate directly in front of the seat. Those were flanked by rowing gates fixed into the bulwarks on either side into which the oars could be fitted and on which they pivoted, identical to those you would see used in the Oxford and Cambridge boat race. They look ridiculously flimsy for the job, but in almost twenty thousand miles at sea in

ocean rowing boats I've never had to replace one. The rowing positions were to some degree adjustable, so you could, in a two-man
team, row together or, in rough weather, move the position closer to
the cabin for more protection.

The sliding rowing seat was where I spent the vast majority of
my time on board, sixteen to twenty hours a day on average as a solo
rower, seven days a week. On occasion, if the situation dictated, I'd
be there around the clock, sliding forward and backward, come rain
or shine, wind or hail, hauling my boat across the North Pacific one
stroke at a time. If the cabin was the nerve center of the boat, the rowing deck was the engine room, an exhausting and often torturous one
at that.

Forward of the rowing deck, forming the foc'sle or front of the
boat, was a smaller version of the aft cabin. Entry was via an identical watertight hatch, but the interior was much lower and narrower,
tapering away sharply to form the cutting edge of the bow. In practical terms, it was nothing more than an easily accessible and spacious
locker, where I could keep equipment that either was bulky or I used
regularly.

For all its special features and design, and despite my considerable experience, my boat and I were now in a desperate, life-
threatening situation. The boat was dead in the water, lying on her
starboard side. The cabin was partially flooded with seawater, which
had rushed in before I'd managed to secure the hatch. As a result,
and with no way of getting rid of that water, there was little hope of
completing the self-righting action the boat was designed for, despite
my continual frenzied attempts to rush at the walls.

The invading salt water had almost certainly contaminated, if
not destroyed, most of my electrical equipment. The two 12-volt batteries at the heart of my power system, whether flooded or not, were
now submerged inside their lockers. Even the isolation switch, which

might at least help protect any undamaged electrical equipment, should I be able to operate it, was out of reach. It, too, was situated inside the now-inaccessible battery locker.

I was sitting in about six inches of freezing cold water, which was sloshing around the inside of the cabin in response to the awkward movements of my now-crippled vessel. The sea level outside was halfway up the main hatch to my right, and the small hatch at the back of the cabin roof, to my left, was completely under water. Exit via either hatch, my only two options for escape, would result in the total flooding of the cabin. Not only that, the moment I opened either hatch, the freezing waters of the North Pacific would rush in and the boat would immediately turn turtle and begin to slowly sink.

To make matters worse—if that were possible—there would be no way to get out safely past that inrush of water until it had stopped. I would have to remain inside the cabin as the freezing ocean poured in until it filled completely before being able to make my escape. The added frustration through all of it was that if I could only get outside without totally flooding the cabin, I could easily right the boat. Once the cabin was flooded, though, I would never be able to get her upright again.

My situation was precarious, to say the least, and was not helped by the fact that, even as I sat deliberating my fate, the boat was ever so slowly listing toward complete capsize. Weight was obviously shifting elsewhere in the boat in its unnatural semi-inverted condition, and there was little doubt that corrupting seawater was now gaining access to areas of the boat not normally permanently submerged. Steadily, the increasing pendulum effect was hauling me toward disaster. One way or another, my boat was going to capsize and effectively sink. It wasn't a matter of if, it was a matter of when.

Despite the chaotic turn of events, I was relieved that I had at least managed to remain relatively calm under the circumstances.

Through the shock and trauma of the capsize, I'd reacted as swiftly and effectively as possible, securing the partially closed hatch and trying to aid the ill-fated self-righting momentum of the boat. Adrenaline had given me the impetus and energy to react to the situation, and I'd done so in a positive way. The fact that I was at least coping effectively with the situation was one ray of sunshine in what was otherwise shaping up to be a very bleak day indeed.

SURVIVAL

Once the initial shock of capsize had subsided and the situation, at least to some degree, was stabilized, I rapidly came to terms with my position. The boat was crippled, on her side, semiflooded, and I was trapped inside the cabin. The only way to right her was to get outside the cabin. My only possible exits through either of my two cabin hatches would flood the cabin immediately, with the boat instantly turning turtle. Her sealed compartment structure would ensure that she remained partially afloat even when completely inverted, but that would be small consolation.

I knew I was in a survival situation and that the row was over in terms of reaching San Francisco. My only goal now was to stay alive long enough for rescue to arrive, if it ever did.

For me there was no emotion or drama accompanying that realization, no overwhelming feeling of fear, crushing defeat, or even self-pity, as one might expect. In fact, I was reinvigorated by my new mission: Stay alive! Survive!

I had a new battle, an immediate short-term battle, and every ounce of my being was gearing up to win it. Whatever coping mechanisms the Royal Marines had taught me all those years ago, it appeared that they were still intact. If I was going to die, I would do so fighting.

Working purely on instinct, I prioritized my tasks and put all of my efforts into surviving. Panic and self-pity would have killed me as surely as anything the North Pacific had in store for me, so I gave space and time to neither.

My immediate thought was that if I could stay alive for four days, there was every chance of rescue arriving. That became my new goal: staying alive for four days. I'm not sure why I focused on four days, but it probably was something I had learned on some long-forgotten sea survival course. From that moment on, every action I took was with a view to surviving long enough for rescue to arrive. If people were going to put themselves at risk to come to my aid, which they invariably would once a Mayday signal was picked up, I was going to make sure their efforts weren't in vain. If they didn't arrive in four days, well, then, I'd just find a way to survive longer.

The first thing I had to do was send an emergency signal. Having lost my long-range communications early in the row, I had only one form of dedicated long-range emergency communication available on board. It was a battery-operated satellite device called an emergency position-indicating radio beacon, or EPIRB. Its function was just what it said on its plastic housing: to indicate my position in an emergency, which this most certainly was.

Fortunately for me, on that morning filled with misfortune, the EPIRB was inside the cabin with me, in my "emergency grab bag." I took it out, released the built-in flexible aerial on the top, pushed back the safety cover, and, flicking the distress switch fully over to the Mayday position, activated the unit. An array of lights of various colors and patterns flashed in sequence, precisely as they were meant to, as the beacon sprang into life, accompanied by a couple of reassuring beeps. Finally, a pulsating strobe light began to flash rhythmically on the top of the unit, like a visual heartbeat.

On the upside, everything appeared to be working as it should; on the downside, there was no way for me to know, despite all the flashing lights and beeps from my enthusiastic yellow friend, whether the signal being emitted was actually being picked up by anyone. In fact, my principal concern at that time was whether the signal would be able to penetrate the walls of my cabin. In the meantime, there was little I could do about that except hope.

As I sat trapped in what was effectively the wreckage of my North Pacific rowing expedition, I asked myself a simple question out loud. (With no communication with the outside world for more than four months, I'd been talking out loud to myself for quite a while.)

"Am I going to die today?"

My response was immediate and unequivocal: "No! Not today! I'm not going to die today."

Hearing those words echo around the cabin, even if they were in my own voice, seemed to give them enormous power, boosting my morale, focusing my mind, and confirming that I wasn't finished yet. Full of resolve, I got down to the daunting task of making that statement a reality.

As bad as my position was, it could have been much worse. Along with my EPIRB, almost all of my other emergency equipment was also inside the cabin with me. I had my waterproof grab bag, which contained a VHF short-range radio, emergency flares, food, water, and medical supplies. I also had my life raft, a one-man version designed for ditching aircrew.

I'd thought about the merits of taking a one-man life raft instead of a four-man one. Finally I'd decided that the one-man version was, though not without its drawbacks, the better option. It would be less bulky and more practical for a solo rower to stow and operate. The question now was, if and when I deployed it, how well would it protect me from the harsh conditions of the North Pacific and for how long?

Alongside my EPIRB, life raft, and grab bag, I had a survival suit stowed in the cabin. It was, after the EPIRB, the most important piece of life-saving equipment on board. First putting on as many layers of dry clothing as I had, hampered by the restrictive confines of my semiaquatic, semi-inverted prison, I wrestled awkwardly into that crucial piece of survival equipment.

It was effectively a dry suit, yellow with reflective strips and with black rubber mittens and socks. A hood helped create what was a nearly watertight seal once the zipper at the front was fully closed. Combined with the multiple layers of dry, heat-preserving clothing I'd put on underneath, the suit would extend my survival in the freezing waters of the North Pacific from possibly minutes to potentially days.

Having won the battle to don my survival suit, finally I put on my life jacket, uninflated at that point so as to allow for an unrestricted exit from the cabin, just as they say in those preflight safety demonstrations we all ignore before airplane takeoff. The cabin would have to be full of water before I could make any escape. An inflated life jacket in that situation would be suicide, as I would be trapped at the top of the cabin when it filled, unable to swim out. I was, I felt, in as strong a position as I could wish for under the circumstances.

If I could stay alive for four days, rescue would arrive. I was certain of it—providing, of course, that my distress signal was being received.

With everything in place in my cabin to maximize my chance of surviving those four days, I now had some important decisions to make, the most important of which was: Should I stay in the cabin or attempt to get out?

Despite the boat's unnatural and seemingly precarious position in the water, lying on her side, I felt relatively secure inside. I was protected from the elements, and water was no longer entering the cabin, as far as I could tell. However, it was apparent that my boat was increasingly listing toward a full capsize.

To compound matters, there was the continued nagging doubt in my mind as to whether my EPIRB signal was actually being received from inside the cabin. There was no question that a signal would be picked up by a satellite if the EPIRB had a clear view of the sky from outside.

On the deck, I also had two battery-operated tracking beacons. They were Argos beacons, which looked like bulkier versions of the EPIRB. They were part of a French-made battery-operated tracking system that automatically updated my position every few hours. Despite my lost communications on day 12, my position and progress had thus been relayed to my family and support team back home throughout the voyage. They would therefore be aware of my position but not of my current predicament.

One unit was turned off. I had been planning to use it later in the trip, when the other Argos beacon's battery ran out. A third unit had already exhausted its power and was lying dead in the forward locker. Crucially, both working units had an SOS alert capability.

If I exited the cabin, switched on both of the Argos beacons, and activated their SOS alerts, there was almost no question that one if not both signals would get through. At the same time, being outside of the cabin would allow my EPIRB signal an unobstructed path to the device's orbiting satellites. It was a compelling argument for deserting the reassuring security of the cabin.

I'd capsized shortly after breakfast, not long after sunrise. By lunchtime my boat was continuing to edge toward full inversion. My big fear was that it would occur during the following night and I would find myself forced to exit the cabin with little warning and in the dark.

Finally I made my decision: I would remain in the cabin until daylight began to fade later that afternoon; then I'd make my escape just before dark. That would allow me to exit at a time of my choosing and with at least some level of control and establish myself in my life raft safely. Or so I thought.

As I mentioned in describing my preparations to film just before disaster struck, one of my principal reasons for returning to the North Pacific had been to record the voyage and bring the story back.

The North Pacific had been a revelation to me on my first attempt the year before: dramatic, vast, beautiful, and teeming with wildlife, particularly whales. But at the same time it embodied a brooding menace. I wanted to bring back a unique and definitive filmed record of that vast stretch of ocean, filmed from the deck of a rowing boat. Bringing back the story was the most important part of the whole project to me, in itself even more important than actually completing the row, as ridiculous as that sounds. The row was the price I had to pay to tell the story, and it was one I was more than willing to pay.

I'd even enrolled at Brighton Film School prior to departure to develop the filmmaking skills I'd need en route. Franz von Habsburg, the owner of the film school, and Maurice Stevens, one of the tutors there, would have been pleased to know that throughout the 109 days leading up to my current dilemma I'd filmed everything. In fact, with the loss of communications in the early stages of the row, filming and documenting the trip had taken on an even greater significance.

I had developed a bizarre, weekly "shaving video selfie" (before selfies were a thing), where I'd use the video screen of my camera as a shaving mirror. Every seven days or so, I'd record a summary of the previous week's adventures while removing the latest crop of stubble from my chin. It became a fixed and highly enjoyable part of my routine. I filmed everything. Every aspect of my daily life on board, however mundane, along with the dramatic and sudden extremes of weather and, on occasion, some enormously raw emotional outpourings.

Above all, I recorded the wildlife encounters. Whales, particularly killer whales, had become a major part of the voyage. Close encounters with those remarkable animals and any number of other species of whale became a thrilling part of the voyage; from pilot whales to sei whales, fin whales, and sperm whales and even one spectacular morning rowing alongside an enormous blue whale, I filmed all of these breathtaking encounters from the deck of my rowing boat.

Strangely, although not as dramatic as the whales, the bird life took on a huge significance. Once you're away from shore a few hundred miles, you lose most of the birds that we normally consider "sea birds." In truth, they're coastal birds. In general, the only birds you see once you are truly at sea are albatrosses and storm petrels.

Albatrosses are huge, graceful birds, at least while they're in the air; they tend to loose some dignity when landing or taking off. Storm petrels are tiny in comparison, not much bigger than a sparrow. Those hardy little creatures accompanied me almost all of the way across the Pacific. They were generally on the wing, but often, particularly after a big storm, I would find them crashed and exhausted on the deck of my boat, recovering. I grew hugely attached to them and at one point had six of the little guys huddled at various points on the boat.

It became such a regular occurrence that I worked out a launch procedure for them when they were ready to take to the air again. I didn't want to injure them with the rowing seat going forward and back, so when they recovered enough to start walking around the deck, I'd pick them up and place them on the upturned bucket in front of my rowing position (my toilet). There they'd invariably sit for a minute, stretching their wings out to dry their feathers before suddenly taking off. I loved it, so much so that on one occasion when I picked the latest recovery victim up, I stopped to film him in my hand and take a picture. Unfortunately, as I did so the boat rocked violently to one side and I inadvertently threw the tiny bird over the side and straight into the water. I was horrified, as I'd never seen the birds on the surface of the ocean before. I thought I'd killed it. I jumped forward and, leaning over the side of my rowing boat, managed to scoop the little fellow out of the water. He landed on the top of the bulwark at the edge of the boat, shook his head, then promptly walked backward, not unlike Michael Jackson doing the moonwalk, and fell straight back into the ocean.

I spent the next forty minutes trying to get back to save that tiny bird flapping about on the surface of the Pacific. Eventually and much to my relief, it managed to become airborne without my help. It was an indication of just how attached I was becoming to my little visitors and the significance they held for me on my lonely voyage. It also provided more unique and irreplaceable footage from a quite incredible voyage.

My attitude to filming remained exactly the same despite the dramatic turn of events when I capsized. During the turmoil of the initial roll, I'd been preoccupied with averting disaster. As soon as the immediate threat was under control, my first instinct was to reach for the camera.

The primary reason for that, I think, was that filming had become such a natural part of everything I did on the boat. Regardless of the situation, it was my natural reaction to record it. Still, as the situation developed and I spoke into the camera, detailing my situation and my actions, I realized that there was added significance to filming my predicament.

For one thing, it would serve as an invaluable source of information to any rescuer who might find the camera before they found me, should I be separated from the boat and the grab bag for any unforeseen reason. Creating a full visual "situation report" could only help any potential rescuer. Detailing the fact that I was in a survival suit, relatively dry with warm kit on underneath, with a life raft and all my survival equipment with me, uninjured and motivated, would be invaluable information to rescuers and crucially could extend the time frame of any search operation that might be mounted.

The report I created was comprehensive, a detailed military-style breakdown of my situation and the actions I'd taken to survive. I explained my decision to exit the cabin before nightfall and the reasons for that decision. I also put on record my state of mind, the gist of it being my mantra: I'm not going to die today.

As certain as I was in my own mind that I was going to survive, one thought did occur to me. With the prospect of opening the hatch to the freezing waters of the North Pacific looming ever nearer and the course of events that would unleash, there was a very real chance, no matter how positive I was, that I might not make it. In acknowledging that reality, I began to understand the immense significance of the footage I was recording. It might be the last communication I would ever make to my family and loved ones.

What should I say? Should I put on a brave or sad face, sound remorseful or try to be cheerful? I decided I would be totally honest, and that became all that mattered.

My family and friends were the people who'd made my North Pacific rows possible, not to mention my previous row across the Atlantic. Without their support, constant enthusiasm, and belief, I'd never have made it to the start line of the Atlantic crossing with my brother, Steve, let alone to this seemingly doomed attempt to cross the North Pacific. If I wasn't going to make it home, it suddenly became very important to me that at least a message would.

The sun was dropping lower on the limited stretch of the horizon I could see from my waterlogged cell. The time for the dreaded but inevitable exit from the cabin was looming ever closer. Everything was in place. As well as my safety equipment, I'd waterproofed the dozens of minicassettes of the precious film footage I'd taken during the voyage and packed them securely inside my watertight grab bag.

I had something like seventy hours of footage recorded. Even if I'd failed in my rowing goals, I had not failed in my filming ones. I had painstakingly and honestly catalogued without doubt what had been the most remarkable four and a half months of my life. That to my mind priceless footage had such significance for me that if I'd been told at that point that either I or the footage would survive but not both, I think I'd have struggled to make the choice.

With the film stowed safely, I began to prepare myself mentally for the enormous step I was about to take. Placing a couple of small bottles of water, some energy bars, and a few spare emergency flares inside my survival suit, I pulled down a couple of pictures of loved ones from the cabin walls and tucked them inside my clothing. The only value the pictures had was to boost my morale, but in my situation morale was a high-value currency. The last thing I placed inside my survival suit was a small piece of driftwood, given to me by a guy named Roger Whitehouse at the start of my first ocean rowing adventure, the 2001 Ward Evans Atlantic Rowing Race from Tenerife to Barbados, which I had successfully completed with my brother, Steve.

Roger had handed it to me just before our departure after what had been a chaotic buildup to the race, saying that it looked like a bird or a whale, depending on your perspective. He hoped it would always signify overcoming adversity, something he felt that Steve and I had demonstrated by just getting to the start line. As I slipped it inside my suit three years later, I very much hoped that he was right. I did a final, nervous check of my preparations and equipment, and then, before opening the hatch, I picked up my waterproof camera and recorded a final message to the people I loved back home.

"Right," I began, bizarrely looking into my own eyes staring back from the reversed camera screen.

"Everything's ready, and I'm about to open the hatch, swim out, and set myself up in the life raft outside. The boat's going to roll over completely soon, and I don't want to be trapped in here having to get out in the dark. I am confident I'm going to survive. I couldn't be in a stronger position to come through this. However, I want you all to know if something does go wrong, I have no regrets. If I don't make it out of this, it was my time to go. If I'd been home, I'd have been hit by a bus.

"This has been the most incredible experience of my life in the most incredible place in the world, and none of it would have been possible without your help. Thank you all. I love you."

That moment was the highest level of self-awareness I'd ever experienced, and it would eventually be the moment I'd look back on that would convince me to return to the North Pacific once more.

My last words to the camera were "Okay, I'm going to open the hatch now. Wish me luck, and I'll see you later." As I switched off the camera, a bizarre thought occurred to me: it was quite possible that if this went badly, the last face I would ever see would be my own.

I attached the waterproofed camera to my grab bag alongside my flashing EPIRB and grabbed hold of the life raft with the same hand. I took a couple of deep breaths, steadying myself for what I was about to do, then reached for the handle on the hatch with my free hand. Twisting the handle downward, I pushed open the hatch, instantly allowing the freezing waters of the North Pacific to rush in, engulfing me and turning my world to chaos.

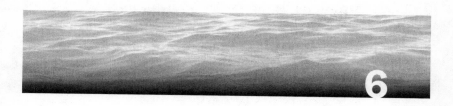

6

OUT OF THE
FRYING PAN . . .

AS THE WATERS of the Pacific roared into the cabin of my tiny boat, she immediately lurched violently toward a complete capsize, plunging me into semidarkness as the cabin disappeared beneath the surface of the water with me trapped inside.

The ocean was ice cold and instantly took my breath away. I fought frantically to deal with the bedlam created inside as the boat rapidly turned turtle. At the same time, I was trying to control my desperate breathing.

It's a natural reaction for the body to go into cold-water shock and cause the lungs to gasp for air when suddenly immersed in cold water. It's one of the principal causes of drowning when people jump off sinking ships; they automatically inhale as a reflex to the cold water as they're submerged. Being a professional sailor, I was well aware of that, but it still took a supreme effort not to give in to that physiological response. It was especially difficult because that response was being fueled by the mounting panic that had threatened to engulf me from the moment the terrifying flood of water had begun roaring through the hatch.

It was mayhem inside the boat as the now-unstoppable flow of bitterly cold salt water streamed in around me. I knew that the boat wouldn't sink completely; the multiple sealed compartments built into the hull would prevent that. But from the second the torrent of freezing water came pouring through the hatch, rational thought disappeared. The "panicked" section of my brain was convinced that the boat was going to sink immediately to the bottom of the ocean, which at that point was four miles below. All that part of my brain wanted was for me to get out. Now!

I was balancing precariously on a tightrope between instinct and panic. Opening the hatch was the point of no return, and I remember thinking as I did it and the water rushed in that I'd made a terrible mistake. At that point it was a little late to be having such thoughts, and with them came a wave of self-doubt; strength-sapping, debilitating panic was close behind.

If I'd given in to that panic, I'm certain I would have drowned in the turmoil of the cabin. There was simply no way out until it filled up and the flow of water had stopped. For the second time that night as my escalating panic threatened to consume me as effectively as the waters of the North Pacific, I once more had reason to thank my Royal Marines background.

Helicopter-ditching drills are part of basic training in the Royal Marines. The very nature of the job as the Royal Navy's commandos means that you are likely to spend a lot of time over water in helicopters. Getting out of one that ditches, as sometimes happens, is a handy skill to possess.

During the training drills a section of guys, usually around nine, are placed in a helicopter simulator and then the simulator is dropped into water, where it promptly rolls over until fully inverted and submerged. At that point you blow bubbles to see which way is up, release your safety belt, punch out the hatch, and swim out of the aircraft, following the bubbles safely to the surface. At least that's the theory. The procedure is designed to re-create the forced landing of a helicopter at sea and its subsequent capsize and sinking and to familiarize trainees with the skills that can help them escape.

The training usually takes place in a specialized swimming pool complete with a wind and wave machine exactly the same as the oil industry uses to train its offshore workers. The finale of the exercise is invariably a full-blown forced landing in the dark with gale-force wind and waves to contend with. It's exciting stuff even in the safe confines of a training environment complete with safety divers. It's even more exciting when it's for real.

Apart from the forced landing, in escaping from my crippled boat I was now experiencing exactly the same situation as that of ditching in a helicopter, except that I was alone and there certainly wasn't a safety diver waiting outside to help me if I messed up. In fact, what might be waiting for me outside was one thought I was deliberately putting to the back of my mind. I had enough to deal with at that point.

Adrenaline flows when you do the ditching drills in training. When you're doing it for real, a tidal wave of the stuff is released into your bloodstream. That's great in terms of giving your body the instant "nuclear fuel" required to deal with a deadly threat, but it blocks the rational thought process. At the point of adrenaline overload, the only things you can safely rely on to function efficiently are experience and training. I was very fortunate that in an otherwise highly unfortunate day, I had a degree of both.

My reactions were instinctive. I braced myself against the cabin wall, and despite every sinew of my body screaming to swim out immediately through the hatch (which would have been impossible against the inrushing water), I remained there as the ocean continued to gush in.

I managed to retain a level of control over my breathing despite the effects of the freezing water, and I fought back the panic that was constantly threatening to undo me. However desperate I was to get out of the boat, I knew there was no way to exit until the water stopped flooding in. The key to survival, as I'd learned all those years ago, was to stay calm and swim out when the boat was completely inverted and the flow of water had stopped. And that was exactly what I did. Well, almost.

The floor of the cabin had become my ceiling as the boat turned over, and my face was pressed firmly up against it. My remaining air space was rapidly giving way to the rising water. In a perfect world, or perhaps in a movie, I would simply have taken a deep breath, remained calmly pressed against the cabin wall, allowing those last precious inches of oxygen to disappear, and then swum serenely through the hatch to safety.

However, it was not a perfect world, and if it was a movie it was not one I wanted to be in. As those last few inches of precious air space began to disappear, I finally gave in to the panic that had been lurking inside me. I took a last desperate breath and made for the hatch while the cabin was still flooding.

Although the flow had slowed, there was still a current of water working against me as I swam toward the hatch. To make matters worse, the upturned boat was bucking violently in response to the waves outside, so the hatch wasn't stationary. It was a moving target in semidarkness.

I managed to grab hold of the frame with my free hand and drag myself through. But as I did so, the grab bag in my left hand caught on something inside and jammed. Half in and half out of the hatch, I frantically tried to tug it free, but it wouldn't come loose. Desperate for air, I finally released it and, gasping for breath, came up in a small air space on the other side of the hatch under my rowing deck, holding only my life raft.

Practically all of my safety equipment was inside the grab bag, as well as my camera and all of my precious film footage. I was devastated but had little time to dwell on the loss. I couldn't get back inside the cabin to recover the bag immediately, as the boat was lurching violently up and down above me.

There was a chance that I would be injured if I hung around beneath the boat too long. The bag was safe in the cabin; I'd go back and get it later, I thought. What mattered now was getting myself safely outside and set up in the life raft. I took another deep breath, ducked down beneath the surface, and swam to the outside of my boat.

I emerged a few seconds later at the side of my now-upturned boat, once more gasping for breath, finally free of my watery tomb. I was treading water as I took stock of my situation beneath an ominously darkening sky. I was clinging to the grab lines, which ran the length of the boat's hull, waves washing over my head, unprotected from the elements and utterly alone in the middle of the dark, frigid waters of the North Pacific. The enormous scale of my predicament bore down on me with an almost physical impact.

Remarkably, that insight, although daunting, served to dissipate the panic that had propelled my premature exit from the cabin. A strong sense of calm began to settle over me. The only experience I can compare that completely instinctive reaction to is taking a big hit in a boxing ring, which I often did whenever I ventured into one.

Your automatic response is to hit back as hard as you can. There's no thought, no decision, just an inbuilt response. This life-and-death situation served only to harden my resolve, made me more determined than ever, and without having consciously to consider anything, I began prioritizing what I needed to do to survive. I was not going to die today!

OUT!

I DIDN'T NEED TO work out the first thing I needed to do: I needed to get out of the water, and quick. Having spent more than four months in close proximity to the North Pacific and its many inhabitants, I knew that if the bitter cold didn't kill me, there were plenty of creatures beneath the surface that could. That would be particularly true when night fell; darkness always seemed to ring the dinner gong for the large predators.

If there is a faster method of going from the top to the bottom of the food chain than suddenly finding yourself treading water clinging to the hull of an upturned rowing boat in the middle of the ocean just as night is falling, I have yet to discover it.

The panicked part of my brain, which until recently had been so desperate to escape the flooding cabin for the "safety" of the open ocean, was now eagerly embracing a new terror: being eaten alive. Of course, it didn't help that I was a child of the seventies—the time of the movie *Jaws*. Peter Benchley and Steven Spielberg have a lot to answer for.

Eager to exit the water, I grabbed the inflation toggle on my life raft and pulled it as hard as I could. With a massively reassuring explosion of escaping high-pressure air, my life raft sprang to life, slowly taking shape beside me like a moth emerging from its chrysalis on a superfast time-lapse film clip. When the inflation process finished and the fully formed single-man life raft sat in the water above me, I suddenly realized why the carrying case had been so amazingly compact; I knew the life raft was small, but now I saw just how minute it was, about the size of a toddler's wading pool.

Minute or not, it was all I had, and my survival depended on it. I took a line attached to the raft and tied it to the grab line running down the side of my inverted boat. I was desperate not to become separated from my boat even in her crippled state, not least because my emergency beacon was still trapped inside and that was the single thing that would tell the rest of the world where I was and that I was in trouble. I began preparing to get out of the water.

The black-and-orange raft was no more than four feet long and just wide enough for an adult to sit comfortably upright inside with a few inches to spare on either side. It was made up of two inflated tubes on each side and at either end, one on top of the other. Those effectively formed the hull of the raft along with a waterproof canvas floor. There was no roof as such, but there was a cover that I could pull up and over me once I was inside, which would give me at least some protection from the elements.

I pulled the raft around so that I faced the end where a canvas strap, which acted as a step, hung down beneath the surface. Putting both feet into the strap and taking hold of a grab line that hung from the top of the tubes, I heaved myself up and half into the raft. Canvas bags hanging down beneath the floor of the tiny raft filled with water and kept it almost glued to the surface of the ocean, preventing it from flipping over my head as I did so.

It was a hugely exhausting and slow process, and the adrenaline that had gotten me that far was beginning to ebb. I knew if I didn't get in straight away I might not get in at all. The fear fueled a final burst of energy, and with one last almighty effort I managed to heave myself exhausted over the side, collapsing into the comparative safety of the raft.

Unfortunately, during my exertions to get inside the raft I'd managed to pretty much fill it with water. To make matters worse, bizarrely, once inside and effectively submerged again, I started getting hit with electric shocks. Every few seconds a really unpleasant jolt would go through me, as if I'd stuck my finger into a wall socket. Disoriented and desperately tired, all I could think was that an electric eel had somehow gotten into the raft with me, and I began thrashing around like a lunatic, trying to find it. The panicked side of my brain had once more picked a perceived threat and canceled out all rational thought.

Then it occurred to me: just before making my exit from the boat, I'd grabbed one final piece of equipment, not strictly a survival item but under the circumstances one I thought might come in handy. It was an active shark repellent supplied by an Australian company called Shark Shield. It was a tapering, flexible black cable about six feet long, that I'd attached to my ankle.

It had a small battery pack in the ankle attachment, which was now intermittently blasting a harsh electrical charge through my body via the water trapped in the raft. I'd always wondered exactly how it worked. Now I knew. I've no idea if it would have repelled a shark, but it was certainly pissing me off, so I reached for my ankle and flicked the battery switch to off, which stopped the shocks. Finally, lying back against the wall of the raft, laughing off my panic, I breathed a huge sigh of relief.

Although I was at last safely inside the raft, my problems were far from over. The raft was full of frigid seawater, and I was sitting upright in it as if I were taking some bizarre offshore bath. Despite my survival suit and layers of warm clothing, I could feel my body heat being leached away by the second. I began to shiver, the automatic first response of your body to get your muscles to generate heat when it's on the road to hypothermia.

I needed to act quickly to improve my situation. In the floor of the raft there was a built-in bailing device, basically a hole in the floor with a round canvas funnel that looked like how you might blow up a giant balloon. I untied the funnel and lifted it up above the water level. All the water inside the canvas funnel then fell out through the bottom of the raft. It took me only a few minutes of rapidly raising and lowering that giant canvas funnel to scoop up most of the water inside the raft and empty it. Immediately I began to feel warmer, and the shivering began to subside.

Then I set about inflating the panels inside the canvas floor, blowing them up by mouth through a tube. That gave me vital insulation from the cold waters of the ocean below, as well as adding some rigidity to the raft floor. Slowly but surely, my new home was taking shape. I was beginning to feel warmer and a bit more secure. The final step was to put the cover up and protect myself from the wind, which was just as effective as the ocean in stealing my precious body heat.

However, before I could do that I needed to get the Argos tracking beacons off the deck of my rowing boat and inside the raft with me, so I could activate their SOS signals. Thankfully, they were secured on the outside of my boat on the rowing deck just a few feet from where the raft was tied. I reached under the bulwarks and eventually managed to retrieve them.

Sitting in my now reasonably dry and fully inflated life raft with two large yellow beacons in front of me, I felt considerably more confident. Even if my EPIRB signal wasn't being received from inside the cabin, I felt sure that the signal from those two units would be. I turned the spare beacon on and activated the SOS facility on both of the devices. There were now three transmitters relaying my distress call and position. Surely at least one of them would be picked up.

Now it was just a matter of staying alive until help arrived. Four days. Stay alive for four days, I thought, and help will get here. I pulled the cover up to make a tented roof on my speck of a life raft and proceeded to wait.

THE CAVALRY

AS IT TURNED OUT, my EPIRB signal had been received almost immediately after I'd activated it inside the cabin, initially by Falmouth Coastguard in the United Kingdom, where it was registered. They in turn had relayed the distress alert to the source nearest to me for assistance, in this case the US Coast Guard station in Kodiak, Alaska.

Some twelve years after the event, completely by chance, I made contact with Petty Officer First Class Patrick Walker of the US Coast Guard, who'd been the flight radar operator on duty that night. He remembered the incident well. He told me that he had been standing by the SAR (search and rescue) loud-hailer, waiting for news of any alerts. The system gave instant brief details of any incident, together with an approximate location to speed up the response time. Further information would follow once the response was under way.

According to Patrick Walker, "The SAR loudspeaker system said, 'Rowboat in distress six hundred miles due south.' I thought it might be a joke. Six hundred miles due south is in the middle of the freaking Pacific.

"The alert was confirmed, though, so we grabbed some sandwiches and a gallon of coffee and headed for the plane. As we take off and start heading south, more information starts coming in over the radio, and the story doesn't change, it's still a rowboat in the middle of the Pacific Ocean. About that time the pilot, Colonel Beverly Carter, who is on her last flight before she quits flying to give birth to her baby, says, 'I have to get up in the middle of the night to save some guy in the middle of the ocean in a *rowboat*?!' [I must add that she is a complete professional and there was more humor in the comment than complaint.]

"At this point we were all still skeptical and thought it more likely some sort of sailboat or fishing boat was in trouble, maybe with 'rowboat' in the name. Or somewhere along the communications line someone misinterpreted something. But we were sure someone was in trouble due to the 406 EPIRB going off, so on we flew."

Unaware of the cogs already sliding into place around the globe to facilitate my rescue, I sat anxiously in my precarious life raft and waited. Night had now fallen completely, and it was pitch black. The wind was still relatively light, which was a blessing, but it was so dark I could barely see beyond the upturned hull of my rowing boat, to which my life raft was secured.

Sitting in my raft, I had time to ponder further the danger of sharks. Only the previous night, before the capsize, a shark had rubbed itself right along the length of my rowing boat as I'd sat on deck preparing dinner. Apparently it's a common behavior to remove parasites from their skin. But from my perspective it was a wholly unnerving experience even from the relatively secure deck of an ocean rowing boat.

Now, less than twenty-four hours later, I was separated from any passing shark only by some vulnerable inflated canvas tubing. It was not particularly big or thick tubing, at that.

Any fear that had gripped me during the escape from my flooding cabin was dwarfed in comparison to the dread I had about the very real possibility of a shark attack, particularly at night. I fought a constant battle with myself to keep that dread under control, pushing it to the back of my mind, because I realized there was nothing I could do about it.

As the night drew on, the wind picked up and my upturned rowing boat and life raft began to move around more violently, banging against each other. Then, to my absolute horror, something began to strike the bottom of the raft. With my anxiety levels immediately soaring, I picked up one of the Argos beacons and began to beat the floor of the raft in response to whatever was striking it from below. I remember thinking that all I wanted to do was get as far above the surface of the water as possible as quickly as possible, and it took every ounce of what little resolve I had left not to clamber out of my life raft and onto the hull of my rowing boat, which would at least offer some separation from whatever was beneath me. Then I saw, with huge relief, what was actually striking the bottom of the raft. It wasn't a shark at all; it was one of the oars that had been secured across my rowing boat prior to the capsize. They'd finally worked their way loose from the straps, and the oar on my side was now flailing wildly, locked in its rowing gate just beneath the surface of the water and regularly striking the underside of my raft as the rowing boat and life raft bucked against the waves. It would have been laughable had it not been so utterly terrifying. I needed to stay calm. If I were reacting like that to a false alarm, how would I cope when it was a real shark?

SO CLOSE . . .

FOUR DAYS. Stay alive for four days, and someone will get to you. That's what I'd told myself right from the beginning of my ordeal. Then suddenly, halfway through the first night, I heard the distant rumbling of what I thought must be an approaching ship.

I pulled down the flimsy cover that acted as the roof of my life raft and tried to locate any passing vessel. I couldn't see navigation lights, but I could definitely hear something. Then, at what seemed like treetop height, I saw the glorious sight of an aircraft flying directly toward me.

My God, I thought, less than a day and someone's here. The EPIRB is working! The bloody EPIRB is working! I unzipped the top of my survival suit and pulled out the extra flares I'd shoved inside before exiting the cabin. My morale went into overload, and my energy levels soared. It looked as though I really wasn't going to die today after all.

I fired off a red parachute flare to let the aircrew know I was still with the boat and alive, and as the aircraft continued to circle, I activated one of my two remaining handheld flares, a fiercely bright white phosphorescent flare normally used to indicate your position to another vessel. The second and last handheld flare I restowed inside my survival suit. I'd need that for the ship that would no doubt be heading my way soon, redirected by my airborne saviors.

The aircraft continued to circle so low and at times so close that I could even make out the red and white Coast Guard markings on its fuselage, lit up by the flashing navigation lights. I recognized the aircraft; it looked like a C-130 Hercules. I'd often flown in those workhorse aircraft of the US and UK militaries during my time in the marines. I'd never been happier to see one, though. The back of the aircraft was open, and I could see the aircrew standing on the ramp looking down as they sped past. I don't think I've ever felt so elated or so relieved in my life.

As easy as it had been for me to see the aircraft on its approach to my location, it hadn't been easy for its crew to see me. As Patrick, the radar operator on the plane, later explained, "Once we started getting close to the area and we got lower to the water, the guys in the back of the plane put on night vision goggles, and I got a cup of coffee and started adjusting my radar for the sea conditions. Or what we thought the sea conditions were. It was pitch black.

"We made a few passes in the area, and I picked up the rowing boat *Mrs D* ever so faintly on the radar. Locating a small fiberglass boat in even light seas is challenging. Still unsure if I had actually found anything, we went even lower, and the guys in back spotted Mick Dawson next to his overturned rowboat. What appeared to be his flashlight was almost dead but gave just enough light that the NVGs were able to spot him."

As it circled, the aircraft began to drop what appeared to be lines of huge flares onto the ocean, turning my previously pitch black environment into a flickering, strangely smoky twilight.

It was a surreal moment. The ocean took on the feel of a movie set with all the new activity. I had an enormous feeling of relief combined with feelings of guilt that I was the center of all this effort.

Then, out of the weird backlit seascape, I saw a large, dark shape slowly heading toward me. I had no idea what it was. It was floating on top of the water, and it looked bulky, but what the hell could it be? As it got closer, to my astonishment I realized that it was a life raft. A very large life raft. It must have been dropped by the aircraft, and as I watched it emerge from the darkness, I honestly thought it was on some sort of remote control as it was heading toward me with such precise accuracy.

I was effectively secured in my little life raft next to one end of my rowing boat, close to the stern. The life raft dropped from the circling plane in the dark hundreds of yards away came so incredibly close that it hit the other end of my rowing boat. It was no more than fifteen feet away from me.

I knew that raft would not only offer me greater protection but would also contain voice communication equipment and a radar transponder, neither of which I had in my raft. However, to reach it meant jumping out of my own raft and swimming to it in the dark. If I didn't reach it or couldn't get on board when I got there, I'd be in serious trouble. Reluctantly I decided I was safer to stay where I was than risk making an attempt and failing.

The larger raft stalled, almost taunting me for a few seconds as it struck the bow of my rowing boat, before finally drifting off into the night, leaving me to ponder at length the wisdom of my decision.

Years later Patrick, the radar operator, assured me that the accuracy of the raft drop was due entirely to the skills and expertise of the pilot and the aircrew. There was no remote control. The Coast Guard flight teams train regularly for such missions, using information on wind and current direction and speed to drop rafts with astonishing accuracy. It's training that obviously pays off.

After the excitement of the barnstorming arrival, the flare drops, and the desperate near miss with the life raft, things began to settle down again. The aircraft stayed on station, circling my position but adopting a higher—and no doubt safer—altitude. I knew a ship would now be en route to my position, and its arrival should hopefully be a matter of hours rather than the days that I'd envisaged.

I was still in a very dangerous situation. The rescue I'd been so confident would come was now on its way, but there was no immediate physical solution to my predicament. I needed to stay focused on my survival. I was one man in a very small life raft in a very big ocean at night. I was determined to repay the oustanding efforts of the people who'd so swiftly come to my aid, and staying totally focused on surviving was the only way to do that. I'd be surprised how hard that would become.

10

A SHIP!

THERE WAS A LOT of opportunity to think after the providential arrival of the Coast Guard plane, while I was still waiting for the arrival of a ship. At no point during the whole of my ordeal, and least of all during those later stages, did I ever regret what I'd done or consider attempting to row the North Pacific a mistake.

There was no self-pity, no "Get me out of this, God, and I'll never do anything like this again." In fact, quite the opposite. I was, in the back of my mind, already planning how I'd come back and bloody well finish the row. This was just one more setback to overcome in order to achieve something remarkable.

My principal emotion was anger. Anger at the North Pacific. I'd regarded that particular stretch of ocean as my own personal adversary ever since the moment I'd stepped onto the boat. This vast ocean had long since developed its own personality, as far as I was concerned. It was a mean, stubborn, and at times spiteful personality, which delighted at every opportunity to delay my progress east across its great expanse. This latest setback was just another mean trick in its seemingly never-ending arsenal of mean tricks to halt my passage toward the Golden Gate Bridge.

I remember saying out loud, "You'll have to do better than this to stop me." I fell short of actually saying what was implicit in that statement—"You'll have to kill me to stop me"—as I thought that might be tempting fate.

I didn't seize on religion in my time of need, either. Although I'd been speaking to myself and the Pacific on occasion at length during the four and a half months I'd spent at sea alone, I'd never felt the need to speak to any God. In fact, I remember before I exited the cabin refusing to become one of those people who, finding themselves faced with a life-or-death situation, discovers religion and starts begging God for a get-out-of-jail-free card. "I never asked for your help to get here, so I'm not going to ask for your help now." That was my reasoning.

Throughout the voyage there had been low times when I'd battled frustration, despair, and on occasion self-pity and fear. But never once had I felt alone; in fact, far from it. To my mind that feeling of belonging had nothing to do with any God watching over me but with my supportive family and my loyal friends. It was they, and in particular my parents, who'd given me the confidence and self-belief to embark on this perilous voyage. I wasn't about to hand that credit over to some faceless deity now just because the going had gotten tough and I wanted a way out.

If a God did indeed create me, I was pretty sure he'd have been wise enough to incorporate all the characteristics I would eventually require to one day row the North Pacific, if that was what I was meant to do. So the question of whether there was or wasn't a God didn't in any way alter my situation. Either way, I needed to exploit the strengths and qualities I possessed to survive. If there were to be a get-out-of-jail-free card, it was down to me to produce it. Relying on miracles would have been a pointless and disappointing waste of energy, and it was an option I refused to consider.

I had completely lost track of time when the ship arrived. It was still dark and certainly after midnight, but my wristwatch was beneath my survival suit, so I could only guess at the precise time—perhaps 2 or 3 a.m. the following day. It wasn't as dramatic an arrival as the air cavalry hurtling over the horizon earlier that night, but I greeted the sight of the ship's distant navigation lights with precisely the same ecstatic level of elation and relief.

The flares dropped by the Coast Guard had long since burned out, and my surroundings had been instantly reclaimed by ink black night. But for the first time in the whole of my voyage, seeing the distinct navigation lights of a large commercial vessel heading directly toward me filled me with joy, as opposed to the bone-chilling terror of previous unexpected encounters, when I had feared being smashed to pieces.

Four days had been my mantra: stay alive for four days, and help will come. Here I was, less than twenty-four hours later, and salvation was in sight. I was home free. Or so I thought.

The ship seemed to stop in the distance. Presumably the crew was preparing everything on board for the final stages of the rescue. I would discover later that the captain had been considering the merits of waiting until daylight, which was then only a few hours away, to make the rescue safer. It was too rough to lower boats from the ship, and maneuvering the huge vessel in the dark was fraught with risk.

But he thought better of it, and finally I saw that the ship was again on a path toward me. Two white navigation lights, one almost directly above the other, with a green and a red light on either side told me that the ship was heading straight for me, even before I caught sight of her huge black silhouette.

The ship, I would later discover, was the *Hanjin Philadelphia*, a vast container ship more than three hundred yards long, carrying more than four thousand containers. She had been in the process of completing her third circumnavigation of the Pacific during the time I'd been at sea when the Coast Guard had alerted the captain to my emergency and she'd diverted her course. The stench of her diesel fumes heralded her arrival, followed by the excited shouts of the crew scurrying around the now-floodlit deck shining searchlights out into the ocean to locate me.

I could not have been in a much better situation to be seen. I had almost all the equipment you could wish for to be picked up visually at night. I had a strobe light on my life jacket flashing constantly, a flashlight in my hand, and a whistle in my mouth, and everything from my survival suit to my life raft was covered in reflective tape.

Still, as the ship approached, it headed past me on my left. That meant the black hull of my upturned rowing boat was between the ship and me. I didn't realize it at the time, but there was enough of the hull above the water surface to partially obscure the view of me in my life raft. Despite my increasingly enthusiastic efforts with flashlight, whistle, and my complete vocal range, the ship appeared to be sailing past me, totally unaware of my location.

All was not lost, though. I still had my white phosphorescent handheld flare. That would illuminate my position like a bonfire. Unfortunately, at just the point when I was about to ignite the flare, the wind picked up significantly, throwing waves over the hull of my rowing boat and swamping my raft. To make matters considerably worse, the line attaching my raft to the rowing boat chose exactly that moment to snap.

Desperate not to be separated from my rowing boat and more crucially the EPIRB, which was still inside, I reached under the bitter cold water, grabbed hold of the lines running along the hull, and held on with my left hand. With the ship less than a hundred yards from my position but obviously still unaware of where I was, I reached for my last flare with my spare hand and activated it. Not so much as a splutter. Nothing.

I watched in dejection from my now-flooded life raft with waves washing over me as my would-be rescuers slowly disappeared into the night from which they had only recently emerged.

It was of little consolation to discover later that as she sailed away from my position, she eventually "rescued" the life raft dropped earlier by the Coast Guard.

With my salvation seemingly vanishing into the night as swiftly as it had arrived, I set about resecuring my life raft to the rowing boat, if only so I could get my hand and arm out of the freezing water. I couldn't put the cover back up to keep off the wind, as I needed to be able to see all around me and signal if the ship came back. But I could bail out the water inside the raft. I was already starting to feel the effects of the biting cold again. I knew my EPIRB was working. That was how I'd been discovered. So my only hope now was that once the ships crew realized that they'd passed the EPIRB position, they would head back toward it.

It was strange the effect that the ship's arrival and subsequent departure had on me. Despite the disappointment of the ship's passing, I was confident it would be back. However, bizarrely, for the first time since the capsize, I could feel my resolve beginning to weaken. There was a small part of me, perversely now that rescue was seemingly at hand, that wanted, if not to give up, at least to hand over responsibility for the rescue to someone else.

It was a debilitating, insidious feeling and, I knew, a potentially deadly one that I couldn't give in to. I consciously refocused my efforts. My survival was up to me. It was no one else's responsibility, and I had to continue to do all I could to make my rescuers' job as simple as possible. Due to my signaling for help, people had put their lives on the line for me. I owed it to them to keep fighting.

Fortunately for me, the Coast Guard aircraft was still on station, they eventually redirected the ship back to my position. The first I knew of that development was sometime later that night, when the navigation lights once more appeared over the horizon, much to my relief. This time as she approached, she was even closer—little more than twenty yards away.

I watched with a mixture of terror and delight as the huge bow of the ship loomed above me. I could hear and see the crew, but even passing so close alongside the vessel they still couldn't see me. I waved my flashlight frantically, shouting and whistling to draw their attention, but it was if I were invisible. Finally, when my raft was about halfway down the length of the vessel, slowly drifting by for a second time, a searchlight fell on me and one of the crew members shouted, "Hey! We've got you!"

"Great!" I shouted back, overjoyed.

A few seconds later he shouted, "But we're going too fast! We're going to go, turn around, and come back again!"

That was not exactly what I'd hoped to hear, but they'd located me and they had a light on me, so this was progress. Slowly the ship continued to drift past me for a second time, with me moving steadily closer and closer to the hull. As I reached the back of the vessel, it must have been no more than eight or ten yards away.

Then disaster struck again.

There was suddenly what seemed like an enormous explosion, and a huge wall of white water burst out from the sloping stern of the ship. The violent wave picked up my rowing boat and threw it on top of me, shredding the raft and throwing me back into the freezing water. As the ship disappeared into the night once more, I was treading water with my life raft destroyed, clinging to the hull of my rowing boat. The pilot must have turned on his stern thruster, I thought, to keep me from going under the back of the ship. Whatever the cause of that catastrophic wave at the point where I thought my problems were over, they'd now become considerably greater.

I tried frantically to get back into the raft, but hardly any of the canvas tubes were still inflated, and those that were simply wouldn't support me. My only option was my rowing boat, so I swam back to her and dragged myself up onto the upturned hull. I crawled along to the rudder, the only place where I could safely hang on, and sat clinging to it with my legs dangling on either side in the ice-cold water. Exhausted and freezing, I looked toward the slowly disappearing single white light at the stern of my rescue ship and could only hope it would get back to me quickly.

I'm not certain how long it took for the ship to turn around. Sometime later, much to my relief, I saw her navigation lights bearing down on me for the third time that night. This time she was right on top of me, and as I clung desperately to the rudder of my rowing boat the ship literally ran me down.

It was the only way she could get close enough to get me alongside and also get a line down to me. Viewed dispassionately, it was a fantastic piece of seamanship expertly carried out by the master of the huge vessel and his crew in difficult conditions. I didn't fully realize that as I bounced down the hull of the ship, straddling the hull of my rowing boat like some maritime rodeo rider. The crew were shouting down to me and throwing lines, none of which managed to reach me. Then, as I was once more about halfway down the ship and resigning myself to a fourth pass, a line was thrown that I managed to grab.

The problem was, I had only one hand free. I had to hang on to the rudder with the other, and the line didn't have a loop in it. There was no way to secure the line to me or the boat. Once more, and for the final time that night, I had cause to be grateful for my Royal Marines background.

Cliff assaults are very much part of the Royal Marines skill set. They involve a number of techniques to get troops and their equipment off a beach and to the top of a cliff. One technique is to rope up, or half walk, half climb, up a cliff using a line deployed from the top, pulling yourself up hand over hand. It's a relatively simple and effective method any Marine is proficient in. In case you develop a problem on the ascent or needed to secure yourself to the line, you are taught a very simple skill: the one-handed bowline. This enables you to tie the rope around you using only one hand. The bowline can be a challenging knot to learn to tie with two hands, as any novice sailor will tell you, so it takes some practice with one hand, but once you learn the technique it's a simple and highly effective way to secure yourself to a cliff face.

When the line thrown down from the deck of the *Hanjin Philadelphia* hit me, it must have been close to fifteen years since I'd last tied a one-handed bowline. But seconds after the line was in my grasp, without even having to think about it, the knot was in place around my waist, safely securing me to a steep steel "cliff." Instinct and training, however distant, had once more come to my rescue, and not for the first time that night I was grateful to both.

It was the last in a series of very helpful coincidences that night for which I had the Royal Marines to thank. I shouldn't have been surprised, ultimately it was my background as a Royal Marine which had allowed me to attempt to row the North Pacific in the first place.

As I bounced along the hull of the ship, still straddling the rudder at the end of my upturned rowing boat, the crew members heaving on the other end of the line, which was now securely tied around my waist steadily slowed me and my rowing boat's progress until I reached a pilot ladder that had been lowered about fifty feet directly down the side of the ship. It was basically a rope ladder that sea pilots use to board or disembark vessels when they're arriving or departing ports. All I had to do now to reach safety was leap from the hull of my rowing boat onto the ladder and climb to the top.

Right. The swell of the ocean was lifting and dropping my rowing boat about ten feet each time it swept past, so when I reached the bottom of the ladder, I realized I'd have to time my jump for the top of a swell. I waited, got my breath back, and, half standing on the upturned hull, half hanging onto the rudder, I jumped for the ladder as my rowing boat reached the top of the swell.

My legs were numb, having been in the cold water since my raft had been destroyed, but I managed to get my feet onto a rung of the ladder and gripped fiercely with both hands. As the next swell arrived, it lifted my rowing boat even higher up the side of the hull and the boat smashed into my leg. Amazingly, that impact would deliver my only real injury of the whole ordeal: a badly bruised shin or, as I saw it, a harsh kiss good-bye from my stalwart rowing boat *Mrs D.*

She'd safely seen my brother and me across the Atlantic Ocean on my first ocean row and protected me for countless thousands of miles on the North Pacific, and now I was deserting her. As far as I was concerned, that was her bitter and well-deserved kiss good-bye. If it didn't break my heart to watch my precious rowing boat disappearing into the darkness as I clung to that pilot ladder, the knowledge that every second of the hours of footage I'd filmed of my incredible, once-in-a-lifetime voyage was going with her certainly did.

I had to push that to the back of my mind for the moment, though. I was still far from safe. I was on the ladder but completely exhausted. I began to drag myself up the side of the huge ship, one step at a time. Sensation slowly began to flow back into my freezing legs and feet as I made my way up, one very slow and deliberate step at a time. I could see a gangway high above me, which had obviously been lowered partway from the deck. The rope ladder I was climbing went up directly through it. I could see a couple of smiling faces staring down at me from the platform, excitedly shouting encouragement and gesturing for me to keep climbing.

Slowly, pausing to regain my energy after each step, I edged higher and higher up the side of the hull and emerged through a hatch onto the gangway. The two Filipino crew members who'd been so enthusiastically encouraging my progress immediately grabbed hold of my arms to help me.

Speaking rapidly into a handheld radio, one of the guys informed the bridge that I was safely on board. Then the two of them helped me off the ladder and onto the gangway steps. I was absolutely exhausted. With my two new friends' support I slowly walked up the steps of the gangway the last few feet to the deck. At the top I was greeted by a host of smiling Filipino faces, all equally keen to help and seemingly almost as pleased to see me as I was to see them.

Finally I could hand over all responsibility to other people and give in to the urge that had gripped me throughout the later stages of the rescue. Yet even now I refused to do so. My enthusiastic rescuers were determined, understandably, to place me in a stretcher and carry me to the sick bay. I was equally determined to maintain some level of dignity and walk to the medical center.

There was some good-natured debate on the subject for a short while before a compromise was reached, and with the hands-on support of my original two Philippine friends on the gangway I was helped on my way up to the sick bay on my own, albeit shaky, two feet.

When I reached the sick bay, several floors up within the imposing white superstructure of the enormous ship, I was greeted by the delightful sight of a bath filled close to the brim with steaming hot water. After four months without anything resembling a proper shower, I rapidly disrobed and immersed myself in its warm, welcoming waters. A constant and seemingly never-ending supply of tea accompanied my enthusiastic efforts to wash from my body the filth of 109 days alone on a rowing boat in the North Pacific.

Finally, when the bathwater began to cool and my not inconsiderable capacity for tea was reached, I emerged from the sick bay resplendent in borrowed flip-flops, gray tracksuit bottoms, and a matching sweatshirt. I felt like a new man, a world away from the exhausted shipwrecked mariner dragging himself up the pilot ladder less than an hour earlier.

There remained one very important task to complete: I needed to thank the master of the vessel personally, the man whose skill and professionalism had been responsible for my salvation.

The last couple of floors up to the ship's bridge, at the top of the superstructure, where the captain was still on duty, were beyond the range of the elevator that had delivered me to the sick bay. Having to walk those last few flights of steps reminded me, despite my reinvigorated morale, how shattered I was, both physically and emotionally, and how desperately I needed rest. For now, though, that could wait.

The bridge was in almost complete darkness when I stepped onto it, so as to preserve the night vision of the watch keepers on duty. Joseph, one of my original two rescuers, whom I'd since discovered was the ship's chief officer, guided me to where the captain was standing in the darkness and introduced me.

"Mick Dawson, this is the master of the vessel, Captain Peter Winter. Captain, this is Mick Dawson."

There, in the almost pitch black of what remained of that long, moonless night, a grinning, hopelessly grateful Englishman firmly and repeatedly shook the hand of the smiling German captain who'd just saved his life.

"Thank you, Captain, and thanks to your crew" was all I could think to say.

"Welcome on board, Mr. Dawson. Welcome on board," was his warm reply as he shook my hand.

High in the sky above the ship, and unbeknown to me, the US Coast Guard aircraft finally set off back toward base.

In the words of Patrick Walker the flight radar operator, "We stuck around flying in circles and guiding the *Hanjin Philadelphia* to the *Mrs D* until they confirmed that Mr. Dawson was on board and safe. On the flight home we dreamed of all the awards we would get for this, had some more coffee, and celebrated a search-and-rescue case with the best possible outcome."

WHY GO?

BEING SHIPWRECKED in the North Pacific during my 2004 voyage was one of the most dramatic of my ocean rowing adventures, but it wasn't the start of them. That came, as I've mentioned earlier, around the turn of the new millennium, during the winter of 1999.

Having left the Royal Marines eight years previously, I found myself working as a personal chauffeur for Paul Orchard-Lisle, a senior partner of an international real estate company in London. Paul Orchard-Lisle, as well as being a highly respected and successful figure in the London and global business world, was also a high-ranking officer in the Territorial Army, the British equivalent of the US Army Reserves. His father, Mervyn Orchard-Lisle, whom I also worked for when he visited, was a former Royal Marine officer and veteran of D-Day.

The combination of the bosses' high professional standards and the military connection helped create a work environment and a working relationship I was familiar with and enjoyed. There was an expectation of excellence in all that I did and a workload that was varied, rewarding, and surprisingly challenging. It kept me on my toes, plus my salary was triple the figure I'd earned in the marines.

There were occasions when I didn't quite live up to the expectations of excellence, of course, for instance, when I drove the boss and several high-ranking business associates the wrong direction up a one-way bus lane in Cardiff, culminating in an embarrassing stand-off with a double-decker bus and its highly unamused driver. Thankfully, those tended to be rare occurrences.

As much as I enjoyed my time working for Mr. Orchard-Lisle, I always knew that my long-term future lay on the sea. The best route, I thought, was to become a professional sailor. Eventually I made the leap and began working as crew on private yachts. By the winter of 1999, I was beginning to bitterly regret that decision.

Although I was unaware of it at the time, I was, and to some degree remain, the stereotypical ex-serviceman struggling to adapt to civilian life. If you'd asked me then, I'd have said that the people I found myself living and working with in the yachting world weren't normal. The reality, of course, and something I'd come to terms with only many years later, was that *I* wasn't normal. For the first eleven years of my working life, I'd lived and worked in an environment that was anything but normal. With the benefit of hindsight, it really should have come as no surprise that moving out of that environment would bring with it many challenges.

In the military in general, and within organizations such as the Royal Marines in particular, there's a genuine sense of camaraderie. Everyone relies, absolutely, on the people they live and work with, to the point where the effectiveness of the unit and the lives within that unit ultimately depend on that beneficial codependence.

It creates a culture in which the group comes first. That culture makes it inherently stronger, which is precisely why it has developed within the military over centuries. A natural by-product of that culture is that it creates a support system for every individual within the group. Everybody looks out for one another.

In Western society, except for what's left of the traditional family, the group no longer comes first. In today's materialistic society, it's very much the needs and wants of the individual that seem to come first. For all sorts of reasons, people are becoming isolated. Natural support systems rarely exist to help people when they begin to struggle. I was totally unaware of it, but I was well on the way to becoming one of those isolated people.

Working in the glamorous but highly materialistic world of private yachting, the "me-first" mentality, which I'd rarely if ever experienced among my colleagues in the military, was magnified tenfold.

I hated it. I had little in common with the people I worked with. They weren't bad people, but I couldn't relate to them, and I certainly didn't feel I could trust them. I was becoming increasingly lonely and desperate to find something that would replace what was now missing from my life.

Fortunately for me, as things were approaching a head, I finally found what I thought was missing in my life and, more important, what I needed to replace it: Mount Everest!

I was in Italy during the winter of 1999 working on a refit of a superyacht. One of the few real friends I made in the yachting industry was the yacht's captain, Noel Watkins. Noel, tellingly, was ex–Royal New Zealand Navy, which probably goes a long way to explain why we got on so well and possibly why on occasion we got into so much trouble together. I was working with him on some refit work before we sailed his boat to Palma de Mallorca, from where she'd be shipped to the United States.

A few months prior to working with Noel, I'd seen a documentary that told the inspirational story of an old friend of mine, Alan "Reggie" Perrin. It had had a profound and lingering effect on me.

Reggie had joined the Royal Marines with me in 1980. Fourteen years later, he was acting as a range sergeant on a hand grenade

training field when a grenade that had been thrown failed to detonate. The procedure to deal with this was to leave the unexploded
grenade for a designated period in case it was a delayed detonation.
When that time had passed and the grenade had still not gone off,
the range sergeant had the unenviable task of walking out to the
unexploded device to attach an explosive charge to it. Then he'd
return to the safety of the fire trench and detonate the faulty grenade
remotely. Reggie went through the process, but while he was attaching the charge, the grenade exploded in his face.

He survived the blast but was left with devastating injuries to his
brain and body. He was almost completely blind, with the left side of
his body effectively paralyzed from the damage to his brain from the
shrapnel. He was told he would never walk again. The documentary,
The Fall and Rise of Sergeant "Reggie" Perrin, was the story of Reggie's attempt to climb Mount McKinley, the highest peak in North
America, just three years after his accident.

For me it would have been a truly inspirational and humbling
story even if "Reg" had been a complete stranger. The fact that he
was an old friend magnified the impact. I had already suspected that
something vital was missing from my life, and Reggie's story confirmed it. Here was a guy achieving what few able-bodied people on
the planet were capable of when he was almost blind with a body
that was half paralyzed. It was an enormous wake-up call for me.
There was no excuse for me to sit around bemoaning my situation. I
needed to take charge of my future, decide exactly what I wanted out
of life, and make it happen. The only problem was that I had no idea
what exactly that might be.

While I was working with Noel, I read a book called *Into Thin
Air*, the story of the Mount Everest tragedy during the 1996 climbing
season. That was and remains the worst year for deaths on the mountain. At the time an industry had begun to emerge in the Himalayas

where climbing companies competed to guide parties of inexperienced mountaineers, for a fee, to the summit of the iconic mountain. The book is about how it all went horribly wrong.

I read the book in one day. Despite its tragic subject, I was gripped completely from the first page to last by how a host of people had been injured and died in the most dreadful of circumstances. The cause of the tragedy had been a fatal combination of bad weather, bad luck, and bad decisions. I found the book as inspiring as Reggie's story, primarily because amid the chaos and terror of what had gone wrong on Everest that terrible year, stories of incredible individual courage and self-sacrifice had emerged. The disaster had brought the best out of people. I realized for the first time that it wasn't just being part of a group I missed. There was something else I longed for: challenge and risk.

The Royal Marines had given me an unbreakable bond with the people I served with, but it had also provided something more: an environment rich with obstacles to overcome and physical danger, which are both key elements in cementing that bond. I needed to find that combination again. An attempt on Everest would, I believed, enable me to do that.

Unfortunately, one drawback to my eureka moment was that I wasn't a mountaineer. I did have considerable experience in the Arctic, though, and after the ocean my second favorite place on the planet was the mountains. Over a period of time, with the right training, I felt, a guided summit of Everest would be within my capabilities. In fact, an extended training program over a period of several years to reach the necessary standard might even bring its own benefits.

When I ran the idea past some friends with genuine mountain climbing experience, they thought the same, that a guided summit attempt was achievable, provided I could put in the training and preparation. In fact, most of the guys I spoke to said that K2,

Everest's Himalayan sister, would offer a greater test. The relegation of Everest to a seemingly lesser challenge served only to reinforce my belief that I could achieve it.

Private yachting now suddenly became my ideal job. Well paid with few expenses, it made it relatively easy to generate funds for the project. Saving up enough vacation time or taking a sabbatical to fit in the training and the eventual attempt on Everest wouldn't be difficult, either. It was the nature of the job.

The decision was made almost before I put the book down. This was what I'd been looking for. The creeping malaise, if not depression, that had been overtaking me for quite some time lifted instantly. I was excited about the future again, for the first time in a very long time. I was full of purpose and motivated. The world had once more become a place full of exciting possibilities.

However, as often seemed to happen in my life just when I thought I knew exactly which route I was taking, fate delivered an unexpected change of direction.

Sundays on the yacht in the shipyard were days off, and on one of these days off, probably after a night out with Noel, I found myself relaxing, reading an old issue of *FHM*, a "lads'" magazine that was popular at the time. As luck, or its close cousin fate, would have it, inside there was a whole section dedicated to various extreme adventure races. The Marathon des Sables was one, a series of grueling daily marathons run across the African desert. I was familiar with the event, but it held no appeal for me. Then I turned the page, and all thoughts of Everest began to fade.

There was a rowing race taking place across the Atlantic Ocean. It had been held only once before, in 1997, and it was taking place again in 2001. Most important, the organizers were still looking for people to take part.

If there were any drawbacks to the Everest project, they were the timescale and the potential cost of the three or four years' training

I'd need to complete before I could even think about making an attempt on the summit. Patience was never one of my strong points.

As I read through the details of the Ward Evans Atlantic Rowing Race, it quickly became apparent that—apart from the small matter of not actually knowing how to row—I already had all the skills and experience needed to take part. In fact, judging by the article, ocean rowing was in such an embryonic stage of its development that I would probably be considered overqualified.

I began to shelve my ambitions for Everest, replacing them with plans to cross the Atlantic Ocean in a rowing boat. There was one key factor to consider beyond the matter of not knowing how to row: the boats were designed for two-man crews, so I would need a partner. Who did I know who would be as enthusiastic as me about spending two or three months rowing a boat three thousand miles across the Atlantic Ocean?

ATLANTIC 2001

WHAT FOR MANY is the hardest part of rowing across an ocean, finding the right partner, was for me the easiest. My brother, Steve, would row with me. We'd both served in the marines. By that time we'd both left and were equally disillusioned with the dull routine of civilian life. I knew he would be as excited about the prospect as I was. Now I just had to give him the good news.

I rang his home in the United Kingdom from Italy, where I was working on Noel's yacht. His wife, Sandy, answered. Steve was out so I asked her to pass a message on: "Tell him, when he gets back, we're going to row the Atlantic. The documentation for the race should be coming through the post in the next few days." She laughed, thinking it was some sort of joke. Then, upon the absence of any immediate response from me, there was a pause before she asked apprehensively, "You're not joking, are you?"

"No. Of course I'm not joking. There's a race in 2001, it'll be great."

I hung up. Rowing partner sorted; now all we had to do was build a boat, equip it, and find the entry fee for the race, all within little more than a year and a half. Oh, and the pair of us needed to learn how to row. It was certainly going to be a challenge, but as that was precisely what I craved, it simply served to add to the appeal.

There's a cliché in ocean rowing that "The hardest part of any ocean row is getting to the start." Steve and I were about to discover the truth in it as we began our preparations to row across the Atlantic.

As well as the race entry fee, which was more than £11,000, or almost $20,000 back then, we would have to buy the plywood kit for the boat from the organizers and pay to have it constructed. That would eventually add up to at least another £18,000. It would be possible to build the boat ourselves, as it was a relatively simple construction, which would have been more cost-effective. But that was never an option, as I'd be out of the country working during almost all the run-up to the race. Plus it was one thing to learn to row for the first time for an Atlantic rowing race; learning to build the boat at the same time might be pushing it.

After the first phase of construction was completed, with the boat basically an empty shell, we'd have to equip her to the same level as an oceangoing yacht. We didn't need engines, of course; that would be us. We'd also need personal equipment for Steve and me, along with specialist safety and rowing gear, not to mention food for up to four months at sea. That was before we even began factoring in the costs of getting ourselves and the boat to the start of the race in Tenerife and then repatriating her and us from our intended destination, Barbados. There would be loss of earnings, the costs of food and accommodation prior to and after the row, and a host of other unexpected expenses, but I think you've got the idea. If rowing the Atlantic weren't a formidable enough challenge in itself, raising the needed funds certainly was.

We also had only a short time to find the money, and Steve had the extra pressure of supporting a young family. Fortunately, from almost day 1 of the project, a whole raft of people gathered behind us to support us and make our goal possible.

The Cowbridge House Inn, the family pub, immediately assumed the role of project and fund-raising headquarters. Mum and Dad, together with many of their regular customers, created a variety of events to help raise funds. Friends and family alike generously contributed their time, skills, and often hard-earned cash toward our Atlantic goal. Andy Smith, one of my oldest friends, who ran a local auto electrical firm, effectively became our unpaid marine electrician, fitting the boat out for us, a role he kindly continued to fulfill throughout all my ocean rowing adventures.

In Boston, our hometown, the local press flew the flag for us, and many small businesses and organizations came forward to support our ambitions. Almost from the very beginning it became a community project that generated a momentum all its own. It was enormously humbling to be at the center of that generous outpouring.

With the success of the initial fund raising we managed to purchase the plywood kit and ship it to a boat builder in Cornwall. He was recommended by the race organizers. We had no idea at the time that using him was a decision that would define and very nearly end our Atlantic rowing race.

With the boat construction under way, we handed over the first installment of the race entry fee, although at that stage we were still unsure exactly how we were going to pay the remainder of it. Still, we were up and running and were confident that we would see the project through to the end. So was our dedicated and growing band of supporters.

Steve and I knew that a serious level of either personal debt or corporate sponsorship would be required for us to achieve our ultimate aim. It would eventually require a combination of the two. We also began to look further afield for that most elusive of creatures in ocean rowing: a title sponsor.

With neither Steve nor I having had any experience in the area, I decided to contact my former boss Paul Orchard-Lisle for expert help. I explained our plans and asked for any advice he might have or contacts he could suggest that might help us get substantial corporate backing.

His advice, as I recall, was for us both to arrange an appointment with a psychiatrist. However, after that initial, somewhat skeptical response, a steady and consistent flow of support emerged, both from Paul personally and from within the corporate world. Paul's support would remain consistent through all my ocean rowing adventures and helped create the foundation for all my future ocean rowing projects.

The race start was scheduled for October 7, 2001, giving us barely eighteen months to put everything into place, from signing up to taking part. We managed to raise the money required, and before we knew it we were packing the boat and shipping her to Tenerife to be in place for departure with the rest of the fleet.

As I'd been abroad working for most of the preparation period, we'd planned to be in the Canaries for the month leading up to the race to finish off the last small jobs, repack the boat for the voyage, complete sea trials, and get in some much-needed offshore rowing practice.

Up to that point our training had consisted of endless hours in the gym, not least on the dreaded rowing machines, and, when I was home, mile after mile after mile rowing on the River Witham, the freshwater river in Boston that emptied through the roaring sluice gates of my childhood.

We'd even persuaded Boston Rowing Club President Graham Panton, fortunately a patient and optimistic man, to give us some rowing lessons. Anyone witnessing our tentative first strokes under his tutelage, bouncing off alternate banks of the Witham as we wended our way along it—including Graham, I suspect—would have given long odds against our ever reaching Barbados.

Barbados might have been still some way off, but we did reach Tenerife at the beginning of September 2001. Our brand-new and now fully equipped ocean rowing boat would arrive soon after us. We were the first of the rowing teams to arrive on the island and the first to discover that there was a slight problem.

The race was to start from Los Gigantes, a picturesque fishing port–cum–marina on the west coast of Tenerife. Nestling at the base of dramatic cliffs with the black sands of volcanic beaches surrounding it, Los Gigantes is a spectacular departure point from which to start an ocean rowing race. There was one small issue, though: the organizers had forgotten to ask the harbormaster for permission to berth thirty-six rowing boats in his harbor for the two weeks leading up to the race.

We learned this early on because Juan, the harbormaster, frequented the pub in Los Gigantes that Steve and I adopted as our local after we arrived. It was called the Harbour Lights, run by a lovely expat couple, Steve and Gail, with whom we became good friends. Juan was sitting at the end of the bar the first night we arrived, and to say that he was surprised if not a little offended when he heard a transatlantic rowing race had been organized from his port without his knowledge, let alone permission, would have been an understatement. Juan spoke little English but was a pleasant man, very proud but faultlessly polite and hospitable. Despite the awkwardness of the situation, Steve and I got on with him instantly. We hoped the race organizers would, too. They didn't.

We contacted them the following day, hoping that there was some sort of misunderstanding and we'd receive a reassuring explanation. We did receive an explanation: we were told it would all be sorted closer to the race start, that there had indeed been a misunderstanding but that all the boats would be able to berth in Los Gigantes before the race and the start would definitely be from there. We were not reassured.

Juan had explained to us the previous evening that half of his pontoons in an already almost full marina were being lifted for repairs in the next week, so even if he wanted to accommodate the thirty-six rowing boats heading his way, he couldn't. The race organizers seemed as blissfully unaware of that as Juan had been of the impending ocean rowing race descending on his harbor. There was little we could do in the meantime other than wait and continue to hope a solution would be found.

Our boat was due to clear customs in a few days, and we were told by the race organizers that we could transport her to a small fishing port called Playa San Juan, south of Los Gigantes, for now. There we could safely store the boat and work on her before moving to Los Gigantes. There were last-minute jobs to do as well as repacking her for the voyage, and of course we had the crucial sea trials and coastal training we had planned to complete, so we had plenty to get on with.

Sure enough, a few days later our rowing boat, *Mrs D*, successfully cleared customs and was towed down to Playa San Juan, where we collected her.

The tiny fishing harbor in the equally tiny town of San Juan has a formidable stone seawall on its western side. The wall had been built to withstand the fierce Atlantic waves, which regularly pummeled the coast during the winter months and occasionally during the summer ones. It had a raised rampart along its outer edge, similar to what you might see on a castle, protecting a wide tarmacked road that ran the length of the wall on the inside lower section.

The seawall created a small but well-protected bay where there were a few fixed moorings for fishing boats and a slip or ramp down into the water at the far end to launch and retrieve small boats. Halfway along the inside of the pier there was a davit, or crane, to lift boxes full of fish from the fishing boats that populated the harbor. Apart from a fenced-off area at the end, which appeared to be for equipment repairs and storage of fishing tackle, that was it. There was nothing else there.

The wide road along the inside of the seawall was where the rowing boats would be parked on their trailers until the issues with berthing in Los Gigantes could be sorted. There was no power, no toilets, one café, and we were miles from our hotel and, more important, from the hotels where our families and supporters would be staying when they eventually arrived. It was hardly the ideal start.

On Tuesday, September 11, I walked to the shop to restock our fridge with supplies. On the way back I took the opportunity to ring home and let my family know how things were going. I called the pub, and my mum, obviously distressed, answered the phone. "Have you seen the news? They're flying planes into skyscrapers in America, Mick!" was all she said. It made absolutely no sense, and when I asked her to explain, she just told me to find a television and put the news on. I had absolutely no grasp whatsoever of the enormity of the events unfolding that day. I did as she suggested, though, and walked to a café, where, together with a small group of dumbstruck locals and expats, I watched as the dreadful events of what would come to be known as 9/11 unfolded live on television.

Tenerife and the world were very different immediately after the events of that September morning. The excitement of our coming adventure was understandably completely overshadowed by what had happened in the United States. It certainly put our petty trials and tribulations over the race start into perspective.

Short of seeing a mushroom cloud forming behind Big Ben and the Houses of Parliament, I don't think I could have conceived of a more horrifying or more unbelievable image than those of aircraft being flown into the twin towers. The world had suddenly become a much more uncertain place. The unnecessary risk of rowing across an ocean took on a whole new meaning to all of the crews taking part, but especially to the families who would be sending them off.

Soon after, other rowing teams began to arrive on the island. Our days until then had generally started with some training, mostly running the steep local roads and usually finishing with a circuit in the gym in Los Gigantes near where we were staying. Steve was a fitness fanatic, but we were both at a level of fitness comparable to our time in the Marines. We'd trained consistently and conscientiously for the race; it was now a matter of maintaining that level until we departed.

Training over, the rest of the day was usually spent at the boat, ticking off the list of small jobs on board one by one and looking forward to finally being able to launch her and get onto the water. There were things we needed to do, but we'd allowed ourselves plenty of time, so we weren't concerned.

Invariably at the end of each day, we'd head over to the café opposite the harbor gates and grab a beer and relax before heading back to our accommodation further up the coast. On one such occasion, looking over at the harbor entrance across the road, we saw a taxi pull up. Two young, noticeably pale guys got out. One had a huge motorbike chain and lock around his shoulder and the other a retro sports bag from the 1970s with "Ipswich Town Football Club" written on it.

Steve and I looked at each other and in unison said, "Rowers!"

They were indeed, the first team we'd meet on the island, Chris Marett and his friend and rowing partner, Alistair Smee. As they pulled their luggage out of the taxi, we walked over, introduced ourselves, and invited them to join us. A very long night followed as we brought them up to speed with the problems in Los Gigantes over several beers. It finally began to feel like the start of the race, and the oppressive mood that had settled on us after the terrible events of 9/11 finally began to lift.

Within a few days, other rowing boats began arriving at the harbor, adding to the growing sense of anticipation and excitement as the race start loomed. Unfortunately for us, that's when our problems really began.

Chris pointed it out first when he looked over our boat. "You've cut your keel off," he said. "Are you allowed to do that?"

Neither Steve nor I had seen a rowing boat out of the water other than our own until they began to arrive in Tenerife, so we had no idea what he was talking about. Chris had built his own boat, so he knew how the kit had arrived and pointed out on one of the other rowing boats a three-inch strip of plywood that ran from the bow two-thirds of the way back along the centerline of the boat. It was a keel strip, a strip of wood running the length of the boat used to protect the hull of rowing boats that are regularly hauled up onto beaches. It was of no practical use on an ocean rowing boat, but nonetheless it was part of the required design.

Apparently, our boat builder, the one recommended by the organizers, had taken it upon himself to cut it off. We waited anxiously as more and more boats arrived, checking which of the boats had its keel strip still in place. When all thirty-six boats had arrived, there were only three, including ours, without one.

I rang the boat builder in Cornwall and explained our situation. I asked him why he had decided to cut the keel strip off our boat. Apparently an apprentice had done it by mistake. "Why? Does it matter?" he asked nonchalantly. There was no offer to help remedy the mistake.

As it turned out, it did matter—a lot. When we approached the organizers, who by now had set up their air-conditioned headquarters miles up the coast in Los Gigantes, they told us they would disqualify us if we entered the race without a keel strip. Although they were incapable of arranging a start location for their race, they were highly efficient in rigidly enforcing a nonsensical rule. We pointed out that the builder had been recommended by them and there had been a genuine mistake. We and the other two boats in the same predicament, one of which was also a victim of the same boat-building apprentice, were in no way trying to gain an advantage.

It didn't matter. "You can still take part in the race," they said, "but you won't be part of it. You can race out of class."

My response to that was simple: shove your race up your arse, and give us the eleven and a half grand entry fee back; we'll go on our own. Not surprisingly, they weren't enthusiastic about any part of that solution.

I was fuming. We'd invested so much time, money, and effort in getting to that point, and here we were with a worse-than-incompetent race company, which hadn't even sorted a start line, disqualifying us before we began. The fact that the organizers refused to refund our race fee just confirmed my opinion of them.

Steve, always far more sensible than I, took a more measured approach. Although just as angry about what was going on, he pointed out we had sponsors to consider. We had to do all we could to stay a part of the race despite how we felt—for them if not for ourselves.

I knew he was right, and reluctantly we agreed to do all we could to comply. However, I wanted nothing more to do with the organizers. They were now the enemy as far as I was concerned. I wasn't prepared to waste a moment more of my time on them. I was so angry about their level of incompetence, let alone our looming disqualification, that I knew there was nothing positive to be gained my being in the same room as them again.

While all this was going on, the sole US team taking part arrived in town: *American Star*. With the recent shocking events in their homeland, their participation now took on much greater significance. The team was Tom Mailhot, a world-class sea kayaker and former hockey player, and John Zeigler, ex–US Navy and also a top-class flat-water kayaker. John lived in New York and had witnessed the events in Manhattan from his office window across the Hudson

River on September 11. He had lost loved ones in the towers. He would join Tom later. All the teams in the race agreed to fly the Stars and Stripes on their boats at departure as a gesture of solidarity with our race mates.

Along with *American Star* came a film crew, Bill and Luke Wolbach, a father-and-son team whose production company, Lantern Films, was making a documentary of their race. We hit it off with Bill and Luke right away, as well as with Tom. That proved to be lucky, because as the situation with our keel strip developed, it was Bill who came up with the solution.

Walking along the beach one morning, he bumped into a retired Brit. They began chatting, and it transpired that the guy had just moved to the island from the United Kingdom, having recently retired as a boat builder. Or at least he thought he had retired. Bill explained our dilemma and asked if he would postpone that retirement to help us out. The stranger, a sterling example of an Englishman, happily and generously agreed. He also refused to accept any money for his time. It seemed as though our luck might be changing.

The man's name was Roger Whitehouse, the same guy who would give me the symbolic piece of driftwood I took on my Pacific rows. He was a tall, lean man in his early sixties, quietly spoken, reassuringly laid back, and thankfully unflappable. Yes, he could help, he said. Time was short and facilities to do the work were almost nonexistent, but he thought he could sort the problem out.

We set to work on the boat immediately, gaining permission to use the fenced-off fisherman's storage section of the harbor, as that was the only area with electricity. We promptly renamed it the leper colony, as we dragged our boat away from the rest of the fleet and made our home as the first of the three lepers that would eventually be housed there.

There was no way we could turn our boat over to work on the hull. It was too big and heavy to manually turn over, and there was not so much as a block and tackle to help with the lifting process in San Juan. We'd have to keep her on the trailer and do all the work underneath, lying on our backs. The first job we had to do was strip off all the antifoul paint along the center of the hull, then sand it down to the original plywood, largely by hand. Roger, meanwhile, built a couple of wooden sections that would fit together to form the keel strip, and in turn we could apply fiberglass and resin to hold them in place.

All the jobs would take longer than normal because we had to work on our backs with the boat propped up above the trailer. The drying times between coats of resin would also slow the process down, but barring any more unforeseen problems, we could make it. It would be a functional repair at best, though, and it certainly would do little for the streamlining of the hull shape.

With Roger's help alongside Chris and Ali, whose own boat, *Linda*, had been shipped to the wrong island and was late, we got to work. We eventually worked on all three boats in the "leper colony." Initially the word *leper* described our three boats. After endless hours working in our poorly equipped, hot and dusty new home, we finally came to regard ourselves as the lepers, very much separated from the rest of the race population. We developed a siege mentality, which ultimately probably helped.

It was filthy, uncomfortable work, and each day spent under the boat making the needless repairs was a day less spent on the water preparing. But a bond developed among those of us in the leper colony, admittedly a bond based largely on a mutual hatred of the race organizers.

All of our training time was eventually swallowed up by the work to replace the keel, and, much more seriously, we lost all of our sea trials time. It wasn't the preparation we'd planned on, but it looked as though we would have *Mrs D* back in one piece ready for the race start.

That wasn't the case for the boat next to us in the leper colony, though—*43° West* was Damien West's boat. He and his rowing partner and friend, Alex Hinton, had fallen afoul of the same apprentice we'd had. Only they had an awful lot of work to complete on the boat in addition to the keel. Their boat arrived later than ours, and though it looked as though we were on schedule for the start, it was apparent early on that they weren't, despite everyone's best efforts.

To prevent their race being destroyed, Steve decided to bring it up at one of the many team meetings the organizers continued to hold miles up the coast at their headquarters. With all of the other crews present, Steve and Damien explained the situation and Steve said that despite the fact that we were halfway through fitting our keel, we'd be happy if Damien and Alex and the third boat weren't required to fit theirs, as it was obvious that they were now going to struggle to get to the start line in time. The vast majority of the teams, if not all of them, were okay with that. Then one individual chirped up, "Just get the bloody keel put on!"

Amazingly, it was one of the rowers from New Zealand. There were two Kiwi pairs taking part. They were as near to professionals as there were in the race, and all highly capable rowers. Rob Hamill, an Olympic oarsman, had won the inaugural Atlantic race in 1997 with his partner, Phil Stubbs. The pair had finished in an astounding 41 days, 2 hours, 55 minutes. It was their story of the 1997 race that had been told in the *FHM* article I'd read that had inspired me to take part in the race. Tragically, Phil had been killed in a plane crash the following year, but their row in 1997 remains the benchmark for modern ocean rowing on the Atlantic east-to-west route.

Rob is a great guy and a friend now. He was back to race in 2001, although injury would rule him out just before the start. He broke his hand, I'm ashamed to say, on the head of one of my moronic fellow countryman, who was drunkenly assaulting his own wife on the way back from a bar. That act of chivalry robbed Rob of his second Atlantic row.

With the New Zealand reputation in the race established, both the teams were fiercely competitive, and I've no doubt that competitive edge came to the fore when the rower who spoke up insisted that the keel work on Damien and Alex's boat be finished.

In their eyes, the problem effectively ruled out another potential competitor. There would be one less team to beat—although, to be honest, there were few boats capable of competing with the Kiwis in that race with or without a keel, including us.

What I found particularly galling about this reaction was of all the boats in the race, the Kiwis were the only ones who had deliberately removed their keel strips and replaced them with ones the size of a lollipop stick. They'd actively looked to gain an advantage with their keel design. Now, hypocritically, they had no problem destroying the race for another team who had been the victim of a boatbuilding mistake. It left a nasty taste in the mouth and was contrary to the fantastic spirit that was otherwise building around the race. There was nothing any of us could do about it, though; the work would have to be finished on all three of the boats.

THE START

OUR LACK OF FAITH in the reassurances concerning the Los Gigantes start line proved to be well founded. As the days ticked by toward departure, there was close to a mutiny among the race teams. It was becoming clear to everyone that no boats would be able to berth in Los Gigantes, and the conditions in San Juan, even for the race competitors not enjoying the daily delights of the leper colony, were leading to frayed tempers and increasingly loud rumblings of discontent. There was nothing at San Juan in terms of facilities for the teams. The boats couldn't be left in the water even if they could be lowered in, as there were no berths. There was no power, no toilets, no security, nothing we could have reasonably expected from the race organizers. As families and supporters began to arrive and found themselves miles from where the boats and their loved ones were located, the mood for everyone continued to deteriorate.

The founder and CEO of Challenge Business, Sir Chay Blyth, arrived in town, supposedly to resolve the situation. His attempts to negotiate a solution were unsuccessful and included a brawl followed by his leaving the port courtesy of the aforementioned Juan. As I said earlier, although Juan was hospitable, he was a proud man.

By that stage I would have paid good money to have seen that "negotiation" firsthand. But with Steve and me effectively banished to the leper colony, we had to make do with a vivid and highly amusing retelling of the story from Steve and Gail in the Harbour Lights, where apparently the negotiating had begun. After that, we felt it was safe to assume beyond any reasonable doubt that we would not be starting from Los Gigantes.

With that latest development, a large group of angry teams gathered around the café in the harbor in San Juan, intent on removing the branding of the race sponsor from all the boats. That was principally because we'd all been told we had to display the race sponsor's name on the best part of the boat for branding: along both sides of the cabin at the back of the boat. Refusing to do so seemed like the only way to hit back at the race organizers, who'd failed us spectacularly so far on every level. Ironically, Steve and I, who were without doubt the organizers' public enemy number one, now found ourselves arguing against that course of action.

We'd met the guys from the Ward Evans insurance company, which was the race sponsor, and they were as horrified by the shambles that the start had become as everyone else was. Having invested a significant sum of money into the race, they were as much victims as we the rowers were. Tempers cooled and the branding stayed in place, but as departure day loomed and the pressures of an Atlantic row mounted, a cynical "them against us" mentality had taken hold, which sadly came to define the 2001 race.

It was a shame. Sir Chay Blyth was and is a national hero in the United Kingdom, the first person to sail around the world westward single-handed. He was one of a unique band of truly great British adventurers whom I grew up admiring and in awe of. He was part of the same generation as Sir Francis Chichester and Sir Edmund Hillary. The former sailed single-handedly around the world following the clipper ship routes, and the latter was the first to reach the summit of Mount Everest. Each was a genuine and worthy role model to millions of kids in the United Kingdom and around the globe, long before dubious celebrities hijacked that role.

I am forever indebted to Chay Blyth for opening the door to ocean rowing for me. However, I felt the participants in the race deserved better organization. Much better.

As start day loomed, there came the additional problem of how to get the boats into the water and, once afloat, where to berth them in San Juan. The only means of lifting the boats was the fishing box davit halfway along the seawall. It wasn't designed to safely lower one, let alone thirty-six, fully provisioned rowing boats into the water. Besides, it would take forever for a single davit to lower so many boats.

By that stage the teams had long since given up on solutions coming from the organizers. The rowers began to solve the problems themselves, working together to get the boats into the water and securing them wherever they could within the confines of the tiny harbor the day before the race. Slowly, despite the setbacks and constant frustrations, the race fleet was finally taking to the water.

Steve and I were still in a race of our own, against time. The new keel was in place, thanks to Roger Whitehouse, and the work was complete, but only just. On the morning of the race start, we were still repainting the hull with antifoul paint, to keep barnacles that could slow our speed off the hull, after the last layer of resin and fiberglass had finally set.

There was, despite boats having been launched the day before, still a long queue for the solitary davit being used to launch the remainder of the fleet on race day. It looked very much as though we would not make the start of the race, as we were surely going to be at the back of that queue. Our neighbors in the leper colony, Damien and Alex, with their keel far from finished and work on the boat still to be done, had already resigned themselves to starting several days later.

Manhandling our boat on its trailer out of the gate of the colony was a miserable way to leave our friends and fellow lepers. It was not the way we would have chosen to start our adventure, but there was nothing we could do if we wanted to take part in the race.

As we dragged *Mrs D* through the ramshackle wire gates to join the still lengthy queue for the davit, a 4×4 jeep pulled up in front of us and Kenneth Crutchlow jumped out. Kenneth, a larger-than-life, ebullient character, was a stalwart of ocean rowing. He'd been part of many of the early independent ocean rows across the Atlantic and the Pacific, most notably providing support for his friend and legendary ocean rower Peter Bird. Together with his wife, Tatiana, Kenneth formed the Ocean Rowing Society, which remains the principal record keeper and library of information on ocean rowing.

With his large bushy mustache and dressed always, regardless of temperature, as if en route to or from his Savile Row tailor, he looked as if he'd stepped directly out of a Terry Thomas movie. Kenneth came over to us and said, "I've got a winch on the front. We can lower the boats down the slip with this."

We attached our trailer hitch to the winch on his vehicle and slowly but surely, with Kenneth's help and a lot of brute strength, we manhandled *Mrs D* down the slip and into the water. Finally she was afloat. We rowed out of Playa San Juan just fifteen minutes before the start of the race.

It was the first time our boat had ever been in salt water. It wasn't quite the start we'd anticipated, but thanks to Roger Whitehouse, our unretired boat builder, and Ken and his requisitioned truck, we'd pulled it off. Now we had just the small matter of rowing across the Atlantic to worry about.

As we made our way slowly toward the hastily relocated official start line between two yachts anchored just outside the harbor, the stresses of the previous few weeks began to slip away. We'd made it, by the skin of our teeth and with nothing like the preparation we'd hoped and planned for, but here we were, about to row across the Atlantic. How fantastic was that? A gun fired, cheers erupted, and boat horns blasted. Steve and I took our first strokes toward Barbados, leaving the frustrations and chaos of the start behind us. Our adventure had begun.

ON OUR WAY

THE TEMPERATURE was baking hot, the seas calm, with barely a breath of wind or a ripple aside from those made by the steady rhythm of our oars as we struck out from Tenerife. The fleet of rowing boats that crossed the start line with us soon dispersed along their own paths and within a few hours were swallowed up by the vast expanse of the Atlantic. By sunset we were alone on a dark flat seascape. By midnight the first storm arrived.

As we slipped into our planned rowing routine of three hours on, three hours off, with one of us at the oars while the other slept, the wind continued to pick up steadily. By the middle of the night, we had gone from rowing in flat calm to surfing in front of a formidable following sea, in the dark.

When dawn came, Steve shouted to me that it was my watch. "Get out here, Bruv!" he yelled. "These waves are the size of houses!"

Grasping the handrail to help me through the hatch, I stepped onto the deck and looked back. The sea behind us was enormous, its white waves cresting at least thirty feet high behind the boat.

The storm continued to pick up and battered us and the rest of the fleet mercilessly for the next couple of days as we all slowly and uncomfortably left Tenerife behind. It was a harsh introduction to the realities of ocean rowing, but we were pleased to be on our way and already adapting well to our new and exciting environment.

Sixty-eight grueling days later, we found ourselves less than thirty miles off the east coast of Barbados. One more day should see us safely docked. At least that's what we thought at the time. We had expected to be slower than we'd initially anticipated after the last-minute and less-than-streamlined repairs to the hull. But we had hoped we could complete the race in no more than fifty days.

The repair had no doubt had a negative effect on our speed as well as our preparation. The antifoul paint purchased locally and used on the bottom seemed more a magnet for gooseneck barnacles than a repellent. That meant decreasing boat speed and frequent, time consuming, trips over the side to clean the hull.

With the benefit of hindsight, our pace was slower than we'd hoped for several reasons in addition to the poor-quality paint and hurried repairs. My caution as a yachtsman, certainly in the early stages, was one of them. I deployed drogues to prevent possible capsizes whenever the sea picked up. Other teams kept to their cabins with seasickness during the first storm we encountered. They didn't row a stroke. We rowed around the clock, but with a speed-sapping oversized drogue trailing behind to prevent any chance of a capsize. It meant that two days later, teams who'd effectively slept while their boats ran under their own steam in front of the storm woke up twenty miles or more in front of us. A cautious attitude at sea can never be a bad thing, especially when adapting not only to a new boat but a new sport, but in those early days, knowing what I know now, I was undoubtedly overcautious.

Another problem was our lack of the most precious commodity on an ocean rowing boat: experience. Steve and I had plenty of sea experience, but none on a rowing boat on an ocean crossing.

"The best training for an ocean row is the first seven days at sea." That is another classic ocean rowing cliché, but it's no less true for being that. Nothing you can do in training can replicate or compare to that first week at sea in a rowing boat heading out into the open ocean. There's also nothing that can have more value when you set off in an ocean rowing boat than having done it before.

Steve and I were about to join that unique and, at the time, very small group of people who had the experience of crossing an ocean on a rowing boat. The experience would prove invaluable in future adventures. The process of gaining it, however, had brought few benefits in terms of speed to the passage we were about to complete.

Because of this, remarkably, as we approached Barbados and what we thought would be our last twenty-four hours on board, there was an underlying mood of disappointment hanging over us. Only a few dozen people had ever successfully rowed across any ocean. Before the first Atlantic Rowing Race in 1997, something like 40 percent of people who had attempted to row an ocean had been killed doing it. Successfully rowing across any ocean was and remains a spectacular achievement, but ludicrously, we were beating ourselves up because we didn't think we'd done it quickly enough.

We'd had no long-range voice communication on board *Mrs D* for the duration of the voyage, so we'd spoken to nobody since we'd left, with the notable exception of one VHF conversation with the race safety yacht just a few days out. It had just rescued a guy named Andrew Veal from his rowing boat, *Troika Transatlantic*. He'd been taken off after apparently discovering he had a profound fear of the ocean, leaving his wife, Debra, to carry on alone. That would understandably become the story of the race, attracting media attention around the globe.

Debra successfully arrived in Barbados 111 days after the start. My brother and I were gobsmacked when, as the safety yacht sailed by that night, Andrew came on the VHF radio to say hello, seemingly less afraid of the ocean from the deck of a sailing yacht than he had been from the deck of a rowing boat.

"Where's Debra?" Steve asked.

"Oh, I've no idea, we left her hours ago, she could be anywhere by now," Andrew replied.

It would have taken a herd of wild horses to drag either Steve or me away from our boat, let alone from our teammate. But Andrew had left his wife to finish the race alone! In the near darkness on deck we looked at each other, dumbfounded and speechless.

Except for that one brief but remarkable conversation, for the remainder of the voyage we spoke to nobody except each other. We received no weather updates and no news of the aftermath of 9/11, we had no contact with family, and we had absolutely no idea how well or badly we were doing in relation to the rest of the fleet.

We suspected it was badly. Our "poor" performance in the race didn't sit well with either of us. We felt we'd let people down. As poor as we assumed our position in the race might be at that point, our position on the Atlantic was about to get a whole lot worse.

A major gale hit as we were approaching the northern tip of Barbados. Port St. Charles, where we were due to finish, is on the western side of the island, and we needed to row around the northern tip before heading south a few miles and into the marina there. The storm hit as darkness fell. We were little more than twenty miles off Barbados at the time, effectively running in front of a gale blowing 40-plus knots with a windward shore in close proximity. That meant we could potentially be driven onto the rocky eastern coast of the island and wrecked, a bad enough situation for a large yacht to escape from but a potential catastrophe for a small ocean rowing boat.

We battened down the hatches and deployed our parachute anchor from the back of the boat to help slow our progress and keep us upright in the raging seas. It looked, at least for the time being, as if the direction the storm was taking would drive us north of the island. Happily, we wouldn't be wrecked on the ragged coast, but unhappily, it would take forever to row back into Barbados if the storm pushed us too far. If the mood on board had been subdued as we'd approached the island, the arrival of the storm, with its likely consequences, thoroughly destroyed what remained of our morale.

It was a dreadful night, one of the worst I've ever had in an ocean rowing boat. The back hatch in the cabin had broken a few days earlier, and I'd done a temporary repair on it. Steve, much more diligent about such things than I, had subsequently spent a couple hours of his off-watch time fashioning a more substantial fix.

Even with his handiwork in place, there was a steady and annoying drip through the hatch as we lay sheltered in the cabin with the storm worsening outside. If it had been left to my initial repair, we'd have been bailing water out of the cabin with buckets by midnight. We were repeatedly submerged by monstrous waves crashing over the back of the boat. Our parachute anchor, which dragged us stern first into the storm, not only saved us losing miles by being pushed in the wrong direction but also prevented what could have been a fatal capsize.

Life crammed together inside the cabin, with our dripping hatch and a raging storm, around us, was not pleasant. Our mood was made less cheery by the fact we could hear but not see when the huge waves were roaring toward us, like hearing onrushing trains in a black tunnel. The sound would intensify as the monsters got closer, while inside we'd instinctively brace ourselves for their massive impact. Seeming to mock us, these behemoths would sometimes pass by without so much as rocking the boat. Other times they would smash directly into us, slamming *Mrs D* onto her beam end or totally submerging her. It was a terrifying and exhausting experience, and it seemed to go on forever.

Bizarrely, the ferocious sound track to the storm was regularly punctuated by what sounded like machine-gun bullets peppering the outside of the cabin. Too loud and too sporadic to be rain, which itself came in regular torrential downpours, we couldn't work out what it could possibly be. Then we realized that it was flying fish hurling themselves en masse into the side of our boat, obviously just as keen as we were to escape the chaos created by the storm. Between the monster waves and the flying fish, we were getting some welcome to Barbados.

Despite the battering, *Mrs D* was holding up well, as was Steve's timely repair on the hatch. We were losing ground north and west despite deploying the parachute anchor, but that was to be expected under the circumstances. For the present, at least, we were going to avoid being wrecked on the east coast of Barbados. We'd worry about getting back to the island if and when we survived the storm.

Then the rudder broke loose.

One of the most important lessons we'd learned during the voyage, and a fundamental maxim of ocean rowing, if not all boating, is that having a good steering system is vital. We had learned that lesson the hard way, because our steering system was seriously subpar. It consisted of little more than two lines running from the forward rowing position along either side of the boat to a barn door–like rudder fitted onto the stern. Those lines had now come loose in the storm, and as a result the rudder, free of any support, was smashing itself to pieces on the back of the boat.

One of us had to go out on deck to secure it. Indebted to Steve for the repair on the hatch, I felt this was my opportunity to return the favor. He didn't argue. I waited for what I hoped was a lull in the waves to allow me to exit through the hatch and close it safely behind me. I then made my move. The second I stepped outside the hatch, I was smashed in the chest by a couple of those bloody flying fish, part of the endless number still bombarding the sides of our cabin.

I closed the hatch behind me and crouched low to the deck. It was like crawling into a washing machine on a heavy-duty wash cycle. The screaming wind was whipping foam from the surface of the sea, which in the darkness was making visibility beyond the deck of the boat almost impossible. *Mrs D* was pitching and rolling violently in response to the thundering waves. The only good news was that at least the water was warm. It felt like the Caribbean even if it looked like Armageddon.

The lines that led to the rudder were at the far end of the rowing deck alongside the front rowing seat, the most exposed part of the boat, as luck would have it. I crawled along the heaving deck, trying to stay below the level of the bulwarks in case another monster wave hurtled out of the darkness and swept over the boat. When I reached the lines, I was relieved to see that although they had indeed come loose they hadn't broken, and when I secured them the terrifying slamming of the rudder at the back of the boat immediately stopped.

I rapidly spun myself around on the deck and crawled back toward the hatch. The noise was deafening, not only the howling wind but also the waves roaring past the boat. As I got back to the relative security provided by the front of the cabin, a huge wave hit the stern of the boat. We were totally submerged as tons of water engulfed us. I hung on as the deck, which was now invisible beneath the invading waves, slowly emerged from the impact and the remaining seawater on board began to slowly drain out through the gunwales.

The parachute anchor we had deployed from the back of the boat was doing a fantastic job of keeping us upright and safe. It was underwater, acting like a giant drogue on the end of seventy meters of line leading directly out from the back of the boat. The effect was to drag us stern first into the waves, limiting if not ruling out the chance of capsizing. That night and on many occasions in the future, I would owe my life to that simple but invaluable piece of equipment.

With the deck drained and a lull in the waves, I opened the hatch and dived back into the cabin, securing it rapidly behind me. The difference inside compared to the raging maelstrom outside was dramatic. It was like stepping into a different world.

Steve was grinning at me. "All good, Bruv?" he asked.

"Yep. All good," I replied, dripping wet and gasping for breath.

By daybreak the storm was beginning to ease. There were still strong winds pushing us north and west past Barbados, but they were weakening, and the only threat contained in them now was to our destination, not to our lives. The seas were big, but the ferocious breaking waves of the previous night had been reduced to a more predictable flow of rolling granite-colored waves. Slowly, almost spitefully it seemed, the sea and the wind still conspired to push us farther and farther away from Barbados.

Exhausted, we dragged the parachute anchor back into the boat, hoping we wouldn't need it again. Desperately we tried to row *Mrs D* back into the steadily decreasing but still formidable wind and waves. It seemed impossible, and it was doubly frustrating because after we retrieved the parachute anchor, the boat immediately began to lose even more ground in the wrong direction. Our grand adventure was becoming death by a thousand cuts.

We redeployed the anchor and waited. We estimated that after four more hours of this we'd be past the point of no return and would need to abandon the race. If the storm didn't abate sufficiently in the next four hours, we'd lose too much ground west and never be able to row back to Barbados.

Our mood on board mirrored the bleak gray skies overhead, which were threatening to add a new soaking to our concerns. We checked and rechecked our position to see how much ground we were losing, and we debated whether wind and waves had dropped enough to enable us to attempt rowing again. Bringing the parachute anchor back in too early might hemorrhage precious distance in the wrong direction, so the timing was crucial.

As our time frame narrowed, there finally appeared to be a noticeable drop in both the strength of the wind and the size of the swell working against us. It was now or never. If we couldn't row back to Barbados now, we'd have to find another Caribbean island on which to make landfall. Steve dragged the parachute anchor in for what we hoped would be the final time, while I took the oars.

Slowly, and with an amount of effort I'd rarely expended since my time in the marines, I managed to drag the bow of *Mrs D* around into the wind. That in itself was progress, since previously it had been impossible to even point the boat toward Barbados. Rowing as hard as I could in a sea that felt as if it had taken on the consistency of liquid cement, it appeared I could keep her pointing in that direction. Of course, pointing in that direction and going in it were two very different things. It was a glimmer of hope, though, in what had seemed a completely hopeless situation, so we seized upon it.

We decided I would row for an hour and see what progress we made. Steve recorded our position, and I got down to work on the first shift.

A backbreaking hour later, Steve emerged from the cabin with the updated position.

"How did we do?" I asked.

He didn't look happy. "After an hour rowing, we're in exactly the same spot," he said. "We didn't go anywhere at all."

We were silent and deflated. It wasn't the news either of us wanted to hear. Then I thought for a moment and said to him, "Well that's good news, isn't it? That means if we both row together we should be able to make some sort of progress toward Barbados."

Our moods lifted. It was very hard work rowing together, and there would be no opportunity to rest, but it meant there was still a chance we could make it into Barbados. That was all we were asking for, a chance. Steve cooked up a huge bowl of rice and chili to fuel our final efforts. We hoped it would be our last meal on board. Then we set up the two rowing positions one behind the other and began to row.

The first hour we rowed together into the face of the dying storm, we covered a total of four hundred yards toward our destination. The second and third hours we gained similar distances. As the wind steadily fell away and the seas flattened, we managed to double that hourly rate, and having rowed solidly through the night we found ourselves the next morning, if not exactly hurtling toward Barbados at least proceeding there at a healthy one and a half knots. It took us almost twenty-four hours rowing together, but we had made it. We managed against all the odds to row back and into Barbados.

We were exhausted. Not only had we been at sea for what was now seventy days around the clock, we had both rowed the last day nonstop. We'd also had to endure the ferocious battering from the storm on the final approach.

All we wanted to do was get our boat into Port St. Charles and finally finish what we'd promised to do: row across the Atlantic.

As we neared the coastline on the western side of Barbados, just north of Port St. Charles, we saw a large motor yacht steaming toward us. As it came closer, we recognized some of the people on deck waving at us. Other rowers, including Tom Mailhot of the US rowing team and Bill Wolbach, the team's documentary producer, shouted a welcome.

"We thought we'd lost you guys yesterday!" Bill shouted. "Your tracking beacon had you heading to Martinique. Then this morning there was just a straight line heading directly back here. We thought you'd picked up a tow! Incredible!"

No, we hadn't picked up a tow. And it did feel incredible.

We rowed in the last few miles alongside the motor yacht, which conveniently positioned itself between the still unhelpful wind and us. As we arrived off the entrance to the port, Tom shouted over to us again.

"Guys! Your family's not got through customs, yet so they're not at the dock. Do you want to wait out here until they arrive?"

Steve and I at first thought he was joking and looked at each other, bemused, before shouting back *"No!* We'll go in now!"

A few minutes later we entered Port St. Charles to the cheers of a large contingent of well-wishers on the shore and a host of horn blasts as we crossed the finish line.

We'd done it. On Sunday, December 16, 2001, after 70 days, 9 hours, and 12 minutes, my brother, Steve, and I had successfully rowed across the Atlantic Ocean.

It was a surreal moment. We made our way toward the pontoon by the customs building and sure enough discovered that none of our family had arrived yet. We stepped off the boat, unsteady on our sea legs, and cleared customs. We had nothing to declare, apart from being ready for a shower and some sleep. But first to the waiting welcome party.

Just a few minutes into our first beer, a taxi pulled up, and out stepped my brother's wife, Sandy, and their two young children, Sam and Kathie, along with our father. Dad walked over to me, and I'll give him his due, the first thing he said was "Congratulations, well done."

Then the next thing he said was "Son, you'll never believe the journey I've had!" Apparently, Manchester Airport had been a bit of a nightmare.

The 2001 Atlantic rowing race could have been the end of my ocean rowing story. But the last two days of the voyage had completely changed my perception of the race and, most important, how we'd performed in it. Until then we'd both been quite low, as we felt, foolishly, that we'd failed to deliver for the people who'd supported us. It's something I always say to rowers taking part in the race now: "Never lose sight of the fact that when you've finished, you've just rowed across the Atlantic Ocean. That's a big deal no matter how long you take." We had almost lost sight of that fact.

The storm, which we survived, had forced other crews to abandon their boats or take tows to safety. Steve and I had agreed never to put a towline on our boat, whatever happened; we would always row the boat in and we most certainly would not be getting off the boat while she was still afloat.

Getting through the storm was a tough challenge, but the row back to Barbados, which followed, was a phenomenal mental and physical undertaking after more than two months at sea. When we eventually reached Port St. Charles, both Steve and I drew a lot of satisfaction from the fact that nobody had thought it was possible. Nobody had thought we'd get back to Barbados. They had genuinely thought we'd taken a tow from a passing yacht. It was probably the only point of the race where we felt we'd delivered. Ridiculously, having just rowed the Atlantic Ocean, the last few miles were the only part we were unreservedly proud of.

WHAT NEXT?

INVARIABLY the first question you're asked when you've finished an ocean row is "What next?" For most people there is no "next"; they settle back into normal life with the satisfaction of their remarkable achievement in rowing across an ocean.

For me there had to be a "next." The thought of going back to a normal life horrified me. Fortunately, "what next" was already in place as far as I was concerned, even before we pushed off from Tenerife. I was going to row the North Pacific. The Atlantic crossing had become simply a training run.

During the buildup to the race, I had become aware of two serving Royal Marines who were attempting to row the North Pacific. Their aim was to be the first people to row to San Francisco from Japan. The crew consisted of Tim Welford, a veteran of the 1997 Atlantic race, and his rowing partner and friend, Dom Mee.

I'd followed their progress since their departure from Choshi, a large fishing port on the east coast of Japan. Their voyage had been as exciting as it was tough. Major storms had dominated throughout, and the pair had been set back hundreds of miles off the Japanese coast when they were caught in a huge eddy.

As we arrived in Tenerife at the start of our own adventure, it looked very much as though they were heading toward a successful conclusion to theirs. But on September 17, after 136 days at sea and approaching the final thousand miles of their trip, they were run down by a longline tuna-fishing boat. Tim and Dom survived the collision with no major injury, but their boat, *Crackers*, did not.

It was the end of their exploits on the North Pacific but the beginning of mine. I had been so inspired not only by what they'd achieved as their voyage unfolded but also by the way they'd achieved it.

Humor was their principal weapon, and they employed it consistently against every challenge and setback, even "executing" a teddy bear on board with Japanese fireworks. Its crime? Being responsible for the consistently bad wind direction. Through every setback, they demonstrated an unflappable and constant determination to achieve what they'd set out to do.

It was an attitude and an approach I recognized and one I had missed. Rowing the North Pacific would be my next goal, I'd carry on where Tim and Dom had left off. I'd pick up the baton and put a Royal Marine stamp on the first North Pacific crossing to San Francisco.

Unfortunately, by the time we reached Barbados, one thing had become apparent: an attempt on the North Pacific would not be an option for my brother. As enthusiastic as he was about another project, six months at sea on the Pacific's most hostile route was not something he could put his children through the worry of. (He would go on to row across the equally unforgiving but shorter North Atlantic route in a four-man team.) It would be very different without Steve on board, but it was the right decision for him.

I didn't think anyone could replace my brother on the boat, so I made the decision to go alone. That decision led to my first ill-fated attempt in June 2003.

I arrived in Japan with *Mrs D* totally refitted and incorporating all the lessons we'd learned on the Atlantic. The keel strip, on which the race organizers had so adamantly insisted, had been removed. It would have been useful to protect the hull had I been dragging the boat up and down a beach every day, but it was no use to an ocean rowing boat. The solar power system had been boosted with extra panels and a better steering system put into place, or so I thought. A host of minor improvements throughout the boat had made her more efficient, stronger, and, to some degree, more comfortable.

Despite all that preparation and now armed with the invaluable experience of a successful ocean crossing, I proceeded to make the worst decision of my rowing career. After I arrived in Choshi, I discovered that it would be almost six weeks until a gap in the weather appeared when I could safely depart. I'd left it too late; it was early June, and I now had less than four months to reach San Francisco before the onset of winter. I suspected it then, and soon found out, that that is not enough time to row a boat across the North Pacific. To compound matters, I had increasing reservations about the work done on the new steering system, which I'd had built. Either one of those issues should have led to a return the following year. Foolishly I ignored my instincts and left anyway.

There's no excuse for that decision, but if there's a defense, it lies in the enormous pressures that you find yourself under when you're about to embark on such a voyage. Both financially and emotionally, you feel as if you're on the edge of a cliff. If you turn back, you'll be letting down everyone who's helped you reach that point, especially sponsors, but also family and friends. The financial implications of a delay might even make a return out of the question. So there's a compelling argument to ignore your better judgment, step off the cliff, and take your chances, which is exactly what I did.

My introduction to that unique stretch of water was as brief as it was devastating. Little that I experienced on the Atlantic, with the notable exception of the final storm, had prepared me for what I would have to face on the Pacific. I was hit by three increasingly ferocious storms in ten days. I barely had time to get my breath back before I was reeling under the onslaught of the next. The last of them left me almost eight hundred miles off the Japanese coast in thick fog. My rudder, proving my reservations well founded, had been torn from its fittings. My boat was no longer capable of reaching San Francisco.

Deeply disappointed, I returned to Japan. My principal emotion at the time was anger, which I directed solely at myself. It was my boat, my project. Everything that had gone wrong had been my responsibility. From the late departure from Japan to the suspect rudder, the mistakes were mine. I was determined that I would return to Japan but would not make those mistakes again.

NIGHTMARES

TO ME, my return to ocean rowing the following year, although ending in heartbreak with the loss of my boat, justified my belief in myself. I'd learned from my mistakes, and I certainly hadn't repeated them. There were additional lessons learned along the way, as there always are at sea, but despite the ending I was more convinced than ever that I could row a boat from Japan to San Francisco.

Of course, knowing you *can* do something does not necessarily mean that you *should* do it. As I made my way back to Palm Beach on the *Hanjin Philadelphia* after the rescue, I had an enormous number of things to consider before finally committing to a third attempt.

I had, under the circumstances, managed to remain relatively calm and in control during the drama of my capsizing and rescue. In the safety of my luxurious cabin on board my rescue vessel, that control vanished. Throughout the nights I would wake screaming with fear and covered in sweat, reliving in my dreams the events I'd come through. In particular, I dreamed about the desperate escape from the cabin. Except that in my dreams I didn't escape.

I'd kept my imagination largely at bay during the actual event, but now, safe and out of harm's way, my mind focused on the what-ifs.

What if I had caught my life jacket on the way out through the hatch? What if the ship hadn't seen me? What if it had been a real shark under the life raft? Whatever fears I'd suppressed to get through the trauma of the actual event came flooding out of me during the nights on board the ship steaming back to dry land.

As a result, I spent as much time as I could on the bridge. I was guaranteed company, of which I'd had none for more than four months, and I had a clear view of the sea. There was also a never-ending supply of tea and endless time to think while I drank it. I spent a lot of time on the bridge pondering my situation. I wanted to return to Japan for one final attempt. I'd known that from the first minutes of the capsizing. But should I?

I was aware that I'd been the cause of an international rescue operation. I was also aware that from the moment I had activated my emergency beacon, the life of every man and woman who had responded to my distress signal was my responsibility. What if someone had been hurt or killed coming to my aid? What if the Coast Guard aircraft had developed a problem and the crew had had to ditch? That responsibility weighed heavily on me. It's one thing risking your own life; it's quite another risking other people's.

Around the fourth or fifth day, as I sat on the bridge, Joseph, the chief officer who had helped me up the gangway the first night, approached me for a chat.

"Mick," he said, "when are you going to try again?"

I was taken aback. It was a question I would never have expected from him, or for that matter any of the crew or officers.

Flustered, I replied, "Well, I'm not sure I will go back, after all that's happened. It's something I've got to think an awful lot about."

He smiled. "Me and the rest of the officers have been talking," he said. "We've been watching you since you've been on board. We all think you'll go back. Within three years."

I was shocked. "Do you think I should go back?"

"Oh, yes, go back and finish it next time," he said matter-of-factly.

It was a turning point. I was talking to the man who had grabbed my arm at the top of the pilot ladder, one of the men who had put himself at risk to save me. He earned his living on the ocean and had enormous respect for it. He thought going back was the right thing to do. For the first time I started to give myself permission to think seriously about a return. There was one major problem, though: I no longer had a boat.

Once more, however, it seemed that fate was smiling on me. When I returned home, I discovered that the Challenge Business had sold the Atlantic Rowing Race to Simon Chalk, a rower from the 1997 race, a friend and someone as passionate about ocean rowing as I was. I went down to his offices in Devon to give him a debriefing of my rescue so that any lessons I learned could be incorporated into future races.

Simon had traveled out to Japan for the start of my ill-fated 2004 row, so he knew all about my North Pacific ambitions. After the debrief he asked me if I'd like a job working for Woodvale Events, his company. I accepted his generous offer and began working on a sailing project he was launching and also helping with the 2005 Atlantic Rowing Race.

Most important, I could build a state-of-the-art ocean rowing boat using the molds at his workshops. If everything went well I would be able to return to Japan in the spring of 2006.

CHARMED LIFE

WHEN I SET OFF for La Gomera for the start of the 2005 Woodvale Atlantic Rowing Race, my boat was already built to the first-stage fitting, basically the shell of a boat plus hatches. Unlike *Mrs D*, she had not been built from a plywood kit. She was a Kevlar/carbon fiber weave foam-sandwich construction. Laid in molds, she was more streamlined, infinitely stronger, and much lighter. Because of that, I was able to place an additional fifty kilograms of lead along the centerline of the hull. That gave her a predisposition not to capsize and made self-righting more of a certainty if she did.

She was a terrific boat, specifically designed for the rigors of the North Pacific and with a wealth of my ocean rowing experience incorporated into her. I could not have had a better boat for the task ahead of me.

But first my job was another Atlantic race to help organize and watch, or so I thought. There were twenty-six boats taking part in Woodvale's inaugural Atlantic race in 2005, which now included teams of fours and solos as well as the conventional double teams.

My responsibilities were to help the teams in their preparation and act as safety skipper for the early part of the race. If someone is going to drop out, it's likely to happen in those first two or three days or nights. Having me on hand to tow them back into port would mean that the boats wouldn't have to be destroyed at sea by burning if the crews were rescued. That was done to remove hazards for other navigating mariners and had frequently been done during previous races.

It was interesting to see the race from an organizer's perspective for a change. Everyone wanted a great race for the rowers, with a management structure that supported that.

Some of my new colleagues were the same people Steve and I had gone to war with in the 2001 Atlantic debacle. We all wanted to make the 2005 race a different experience, by giving the teams taking part a well-organized, safe event. It was good that we did because the weather would prove to be the worst the race had ever seen.

As the start date approached in La Gomera, the island immediately west of Tenerife, a deep low-pressure system began to threaten. All the teams were desperate to get started. They weren't keen to be told that there would be a delay due to the threat of bad weather. The them-against-us mentality, which had slowly been erased during the countdown to the start, suddenly came to the fore, threatening to jeopardize the great spirit that surrounded the race. The teams were anxious to start, and that seemed like another hurdle being placed in front of them by the race organizers.

It was a call any competent sailor would make. You don't leave port when you know you're heading into bad weather. Let it pass, then leave. It isn't rocket science.

Still, given the tension that builds up around the start of an ocean row, it wasn't the news the teams wanted to hear. Some family members would now miss the start, as they'd already arranged their flights home, or additional accommodation would have to be found at added expense.

"We'll have to cope with storms like this if they happen along the way," one team said to me. True, but putting twenty-six rowing boats out to sea in the face of an Atlantic gale that would likely drive them back to be wrecked on the island would have been madness. As I'd found out to my cost in the past, the right decisions are often the hardest ones to make. We made the right decision, though; the departure was put back for three days.

When the storm finally arrived, the attitude of the teams immediately changed. The port of San Sebastián on La Gomera was battered by winds gusting well over 50 knots with huge waves crashing over the marina wall. Two racing yachts that had entered the harbor to seek refuge were smashed at their temporary moorings as the storm raged on.

All the teams looked on in awe at the power of the ocean and I think for the first time began to fully comprehend the enormous challenge of rowing across the Atlantic. The experience also served to reinforce their faith in the race organizers who'd made the unpopular decision to delay the start. They were starting to realize something I'd already come to understand: it wasn't a case of us against them; it was all of us against the Atlantic.

The new start date was November 30, when twenty-six crews of men and women finally set off from the Canary Islands bound for the historic Nelson's Dockyard in Antigua.

As I sailed out with the fleet in the race safety boat, A "rib" with which I'd provide inshore rescue and recovery for any boats if needed, I envied every one of them the adventure that lay ahead of them. Little did I know that I would soon become part of that adventure.

During the countdown to the start, it was obvious that some teams would have more problems than others. The most famous team taking part and potentially one of the strongest were Ben Fogle, the TV presenter, and James Cracknell, an Olympic and World Rowing Championships flat-water rowing gold-medal legend. On paper they were arguably the team to beat, but they'd arrived with their boat nowhere near finished. If the race hadn't been delayed, they'd have missed the start.

It was a testament to the camaraderie of the 2005 race that many of the other rowers helped them finish the work on their boat. Everyone did their utmost to ensure that all twenty-six boats would make the start line, including that of Ben and James. The fact that they were prepared to help the team that would most likely be their most formidable competition spoke volumes about the spirit surrounding that year's race. Despite everyone's efforts, though, twenty-four hours before the start James was sitting on the deck of his boat trying to help the resin on his rowing position repair set with a hair dryer. I very much doubt that that would have happened at the Olympics. It worked, though; they made the start, and after a challenging voyage they would be the first of the two-man teams to reach Antigua. They were demoted to second place for drinking their emergency water rations, but, like everyone else in that year's race, by then they were no doubt glad just to have finished.

One of the other teams was having problems of a very different nature. Their boat was on schedule to be ready for the start, but the relationship between the rowers was already fraying. I had gotten to know both team members during the buildup to the race, and they seemed like good and capable guys. As the start approached, they were becoming increasingly isolated from each other, if not downright hostile.

So it didn't come as a complete shock to me when just before 11 p.m. on the first night of the race I received a message that their boat, *One Life*, had a medical situation on board that required a tow back into port.

With my friend and fellow ocean rower Graham Walters, I headed out of San Sebastián in the safety "rib" toward their position eighteen miles south of the island. It was a calm night with a typical Atlantic swell, so finding them was relatively quick and easy. Communicating with them was less so.

The team captain was Andrew Morris, or Mos, as he was known, an Englishman from Newark, near my hometown of Boston. Mos was an instantly likable guy, and we based our quick friendship largely on mutual derision of each other's birthplace. Mos is tall and dark-haired, with a smile for anyone he meets and a relentlessly positive outlook on life. He's the sort of bloke who lights up a room with his energy. His teammate, Stéphane Portes, a giant of a Frenchman, was equally affable, if a little more subdued.

As we approached their boat in the darkness, we called out to them. We couldn't see anyone on the deck, and the swell made it difficult to get too close without risking damage. Slowly a head rose above the bulwark. It was Stéphane, who'd obviously been lying on the deck. By the slow speed of his reaction and the lethargy in his reply, he was obviously suffering from seasickness.

We'd been told that Mos had banged his head and was slipping in and out of consciousness. Presumably he was in the cabin. Stéphane assured us that Mos was okay but wanted to go back to to port to see a doctor and make sure. Mos had banged his head on one of the poles that were fixed vertically from the top of the bulwarks, part of a framework to support the spare oars.

Mos eventually emerged from the cabin to assure us that he was okay and promptly threw up. They really weren't having a good time. Graham and I eventually managed to get a line safely secured to their boat and slowly turned and headed back to San Sebastián. *One Life* and its wilting crew became the first boat to drop out of the 2005 Atlantic rowing race.

Hours later, as we approached the harbor entrance, I turned to Graham with a grin and said, "I suspect Mos is going to slip back into consciousness once we get inside the port."

Sure enough, as we entered the flat waters of the harbor, Mos emerged from the cabin, waving to us and anyone he saw on the quayside, back to his normal exuberant self. Stéphane and Mos went their separate ways, Mos to the local hospital and Stéphane eventually back to London.

There had been halfhearted mutterings of setting off together again once Mos received the all clear. But although the bang on the head had been the catalyst for their return to port, the real reason was that they simply weren't functioning as a team. If people are struggling to communicate on the quayside, they're going to struggle even more under the demands of rowing across the Atlantic. The bang on the head proved to be a timely excuse to cut short a disastrous partnership. I'm glad they took it, as it prevented two great guys making what could have proved to be a fatal mistake.

Mos, who as well as taking part in the race had organized the shipping of many of the boats through his freight company, got to work repacking his rowing boat to ship her home. The fleet was making steady progress, so I helped as much as I could.

By that stage most of the people involved in the race had also disappeared and Mos and I were about the only ones left in San Sebastián. We were eating dinner at a local restaurant a couple of days later when he began talking about how much he'd invested in the project, including money, time, effort, and events to raise money for his chosen charity. He was crushed that now it was all for nothing. Knowing exactly what goes into an ocean rowing project, he had my sympathies.

"It's going to be at least two years until I can try this again. And at least another twenty grand," he said. "If only I had an experienced partner to go with me now, I could still make it this time."

I agreed with him and should have known how it was going to turn out. Mos was a capable bloke, easy to get along with, and an experienced and quite competitive flat-water rower, thus a useful addition to any crew. All he lacked was someone with some seagoing or ocean rowing experience. Both he and Stéphane had made the same mistake: they'd chosen the wrong partner.

At the time my brother, Steve, had just returned from rowing across the North Atlantic in a record-breaking four-man boat called *Vivaldi Atlantic 4*. He had experience. I rang Steve from the restaurant and could tell from his voice that he was excited about the prospect. But his daughter, Kathie, was listening to the conversation. The prospect of her dad disappearing to sea again for an extended period of time including Christmas, after only just returning from the dangers of the North Atlantic, horrified her and reduced her to tears. Seeing her reaction, Steve thanked Mos for the offer but turned it down.

"Why don't you go, Mick?" he suggested.

"I can't," I said. "I'm working on the race, and I have to be back in Japan mid-April."

The only other person I could think of was my boss, Simon Chalk. Another passionate and experienced ocean rower, he was as enthusiastic as Steve at the possibility, but it wasn't an option for him, either. He had an enormous amount of work on his plate with the race now under way as well as running his property business.

"Why don't you go, Mick?" he asked.

"Because I'm working for you and I'm off to Japan in April."

"We can spare you from work, and you'll be back in plenty of time to get ready for Japan," he replied.

I thought about it for a minute. Mos was already working out how we would catch up to the rest of the fleet. I knew we'd get along; Mos could easily drive a person mad, but it would be impossible to fall out with him. He was too nice a bloke. Plus, I thought, it would be great training for the North Pacific.

"Okay," I said, "I'll go. But one condition."

"What's that?"

"We rename the boat *Charmed Life*."

"Why?"

When Mos asked me that question, I told him about my Pacific experience and the song "Charmed Life," which had helped me get through the lowest points. The notion of a charmed life had become my shield against defeat, and "Never, never, never, never, never give up" had become my motto.

Mos liked that connection and agreed to the name change, and we immediately started thinking about how to join the race.

STORM!

WE NOW HAD TO GET Mos's boat ready for sea again. She'd been lifted out of the water and partially dismantled and was now waiting to be packed into a container and shipped back to England. We needed to set off as soon as possible if we were to have any hope of catching up with the rest of the fleet. The clock was ticking.

There was, of course, another problem, the fact that of all the boats in the fleet, the soon-to-become *Charmed Life* was maybe the worst set up. She was well built, safe, and surprisingly fast, but had there been time I would have changed or replaced almost every system on her.

It wasn't a lack of will on Mos's part but simply a lack of knowledge. If I'd had my boat from the start of our Atlantic race in front of me, I'd have found almost as much to criticize. As I looked at *Charmed Life* on the quayside, though, that didn't make the situation any less frustrating.

The first thing I noticed was that the oars were the wrong type. They were great for flat-water rowing, but on an ocean row they would be vulnerable to snapping. They simply weren't robust enough for an ocean row. Unfortunately it was too late to replace them. We'd eventually arrive in Antigua with only one of the original eight oars still intact. The only other working oar was damaged and had been repaired, and, as it turned out, just forty-five minutes away from joining its seven predecessors by breaking in two when Mos took a friend for a spin in the harbor after we'd finished. I had expected some breakage, but nowhere near that level of attrition.

The water maker, an obvious essential for any ocean voyage, was the cheapest and worst option available. That said, it was identical to the one Steve and I had used on our Atlantic crossing. Although it worked to the best of its ability for the whole of our Atlantic voyage, that was rarely the experience other rowers had. For Mos and me, it struggled to supply enough water for drinking and cooking, let alone for any other jobs on board. At best it could produce six liters of water an hour. For my Pacific rows I used a Spectra water maker, which produced almost 25 liters an hour.

That kind of water supply transforms an ocean row. It means that not only do you have plenty of water to drink and cook with, but you can wash regularly. You can also rinse the salt off the boat, particularly the seat covers, which easily become saturated, causing sores and making life at the oars deeply uncomfortable. Crucially, it's also less of a drain on the precious battery power.

The useless water maker had been fitted in the boat when Mos had bought her, and it would have cost several thousand pounds to replace it with a better system. In any event, he had decided against it. That was an understandable financial decision—unless you'd ever rowed across an ocean. I'd spent the previous year advising every team I'd spoken to that they should use a Spectra water maker. Most had taken the advice. Now here I was about to cross the Atlantic for a second time with an inferior machine on my boat.

The steering system was also poor. It was not unlike the one we had used on *Mrs D* in 2001, apart from the fact that you adjusted the rudder by moving the rowing footplate rather than by hand. I'd never been a fan of that type of steering system. I thought it would be strong enough to withstand the conditions, which it proved to be, but in terms of accurately and effectively steering the boat in a big sea, the doubts I had would later be confirmed.

There was nothing I could do about any of that. The boat would function safely, though she was less efficient and less comfortable than she might have been. I'd have to put up with it.

There was greater scope for improvement of the stores and supplies on board. I removed every item that wasn't nailed down and repacked the whole boat with only what was required and useful. At the end of that process there was a pile of excess supplies weighing more than 170 pounds sitting on the quayside. On top of the pile was an oven glove that had been mysteriously tied to the deck.

To make the process of repacking swifter, I'd asked Mos to sort out the all-important musical playlist for the voyage and let me take care of the boat. He'd promptly disappeared to see a local techie he'd discovered on the other side of the island, who was going to help him cram as broad and exciting a selection of music as possible onto his then-state-of-the art MP3 player. He came back to San Sebastián the following morning, saying "I've got some good news for you, Mick, and I've got some bad news for you."

"What's the good news?"

"Last night I downloaded over sixteen hundred albums from artists all over the world onto this MP3 player."

"And the bad news?"

"This morning I seem to have deleted all but one of them."

So six days after the rest of the fleet departed, Mos and I set off in pursuit of them on a three-thousand-mile voyage to Antigua. Our home for the next several months was a rowing boat with an inferior water maker, dodgy oars, and one Robbie Williams double album, *Swing When You're Winning*, to keep us company.

*   *   *

Mos and I are both fiercely competitive, and we both wanted to be serious contenders in the race. With weather forecasts suggesting more storms due, I felt we could be. We might not be able to win the race, but we had every chance of catching the lead pack.

There were only a few experienced ocean rowers taking part in the race that year, and I knew that as soon as bad weather hit, many teams would throw out an anchor and retreat to their cabins. In the early part of the race they would have neither the confidence nor the will to row into a building storm.

We would. Every storm would offer a chance for us to gain ground on the fleet. Of course, that strategy relied on our both rowing as long as possible while the weather deteriorated.

I explained to Mos that every bout of bad weather was an opportunity to gain ground. Even when we reached the point where we had to stop rowing, we could still catch up. After my adventures on the Pacific, I was an expert at using a para anchor effectively. All Mos had to do was trust me and be prepared to keep rowing even when the weather closed in and things became a little scary. In the warmth of the dockside restaurant that didn't faze Mos at all. As we faced the first gale at sea, he was less enthusiastic.

We'd been rowing about three days when the forecasted storm arrived. We were already catching the trailing boats in the race— even after giving them a six-day head start—and our average speed was good. We were gaining steadily, and Mos was adapting well to life on an ocean rowing boat.

By the time the weather front hit us with increased wind and torrential rain, most of the fleet were already riding it out on their parachute anchors, slowly drifting back toward us. The longer we could keep going into the storm before doing the same, the more the gap between us would close.

Mos is a highly successful businessman and a fearless motorcycle and race car driver. But in those early days of the row, I'm sure even he would admit that he was completely out of his comfort zone as the Atlantic showed her dark side. As the wind and waves rose up and pouring rain beat down on us, our speed was halved. We were still gaining ground on the other boats, though, as their crews had all, understandably, retreated to the security of their cabins.

It was exhausting work with the boat pitching and rolling in the building seas, but we were gaining ground with every stroke. Then a wave struck the side of the boat, snatching one of the oars out of Mos's grasp. It bounced back, smashing into his wrist.

He called out, and I went back on deck to see what the problem was. He'd obviously taken a whack on the wrist. There were a bruise and some broken skin, but there didn't appear to be any major injury.

"I can't row anymore," he said.

"What do you mean, you can't row anymore?"

"I've injured my wrist. I can't row anymore."

I could see he was shaken up as much, I felt, by the conditions as the injury. It was almost my watch, though, so I said to him, "Okay, I'll take over. You have a rest and see how you are at the next change-over."

The conditions were soaking wet and miserable with a horribly depressing leaden sky and an ominous rolling gray sea. Crucially, though, we were able to maintain our course to the southwest, albeit slowly. It was challenging, but it was still safe to row. If we were to catch the leading pack, those were exactly the kind of conditions that would allow us to do so.

When the changeover time came, Mos opened the hatch and told me he still couldn't row. He'd taken some painkillers, but his wrist was still too painful. As well as disappointed, I was angry. I had no doubt his wrist was sore, but it was hardly a cause to stop rowing.

He could still move his fingers. I'd agreed to join him with the aim of getting to Antigua as fast as possible. He wanted to do well in the race. I wanted to get back in time to prepare my boat for Japan. Here we were on the third day, and he was refusing to row. This could become a nightmare.

"I wouldn't ask you to do this if I didn't think it was safe and you were capable, mate," I said.

It was no use. He was not going to row.

"Fuck it, then. You get your head down, and I'll row."

I spent the next ten hours rowing before it finally became impossible to make progress. We gained almost twenty miles on the other boats. That whole time, I was staring at the hatch, seething that my rowing partner was fast asleep inside while I was outside doing all the work. That was why I hadn't wanted to replace my brother with another rower. This would never have happened with him on board, and it would never have happened if another marine had been rowing with me.

Then it dawned on me. I was the one who was out of order here. Not for the first or last time in my life, I was condemning somebody for not having the attitude I'd expect from a Royal Marine. I had to remind myself that I was no longer working with Royal Marines. All the others in the race at that point were in their cabin, riding out the storm. I was the only one still on deck trying to make progress. Mos's reaction was the normal one; I was the odd one out. With a dreadful sinking feeling I saw that there was more danger of my attitude ruining our partnership than Mos's.

After I stopped rowing, I shouted to Mos to come out and help me deploy the sea anchor. I had to defuse the situation and make the partnership work. This was about me adapting my approach not insisting Mos adapt his. He was coming to terms with an incredibly daunting new environment, and up until the storm hit, he'd been doing that brilliantly. He needed my help, not my condemnation.

That said, this wasn't a theme park ride we were on. The more days spent on an ocean in a rowing boat, the more chances you give the ocean to stop you. The end of my first Atlantic row had shown me that. I had to find a balance.

When we had set the sea anchor, I said to him, "Mos, we need to clear the air. It's like this, mate. If you break your arm, I'll row you and this boat to Antigua, no matter how long it takes. If I break my arm, that's exactly what I expect you'll do for me. However, I'm not interested in hearing that your wrist is sore and that you don't fancy rowing because it's painful. I really don't care how painful it is so long as you can still row. I can promise you you're never going to hear me say that. This can be a very dangerous place, and we need to work together as hard as we possibly can to get across it as quickly as possible. You have to trust me and I have to be able to trust you; that's the only way this can work."

After that we rode out the worst of the storm locked in the cabin together. He made no move to strangle me in my sleep or club me to death, so presumably he wasn't unhappy with what I'd said. All I know is that from that point on Mos steadily became the best ocean rowing partner I could have wished for.

He still very much remained Mos. Consistently late for watch changeovers, he'd never even heard of the concept of being five minutes early. He'd regularly emerge from the cabin furiously brushing his teeth and spit out the toothpaste, which invariably ended up all over me as he never checked the wind direction first. He was also blissfully unaware that an ocean rowing boat might not be the best place to learn to play the harmonica, at least not from his partner's point of view, although it did make for an interesting version of "Auld Lang Syne" on New Year's Eve. But despite those foibles and being very much out of his comfort zone in an often terrifying environment, after that first storm he never once failed to come up to the mark as far as I was concerned.

I, on the other hand, remained the occasionally grumpy ex-serviceman who was in a hurry to get to Antigua. Only now I was an occasionally grumpy ex-serviceman who showed his remarkably brave teammate a little more consideration. We might have been the most unlikely partnership to begin with, but we became one of the strongest as our voyage on *Charmed Life* progressed.

It was just as well we did. The Atlantic had much in store for us.

CAPSIZE!

TWENTY-SIX BOATS took part in that year's race, six of which would ultimately be lost. All of their crews were safely rescued, a testament to the work we'd put in organizing the race safety protocol and training. A further seventeen boats would suffer capsizes, including ours.

The pattern of storms had continued as we'd progressed, and the conditions we'd endured would not have been out of place on the North Pacific. It was proving to be a good training run for my return to Japan.

As ferocious as the storms were, the major problem that year was the trade winds. They normally blow toward the Caribbean at a steady 10 to 15 knots. That year they were blowing consistently at 20 to 25 knots.

Over time, large breaking waves began to develop. To make matters worse, every so often one of these waves would smash into the one in front of it, creating a monstrous breaking wave that would suddenly and alarmingly appear seemingly out of nowhere.

We were in the later stages of the voyage, less than two weeks from Antigua, when we capsized.

In the first half of the race, as I'd expected, we'd steamed right through the pack of boats. With a six-day handicap we were never going to catch the lead three or four boats, but we were right on the tail of those behind them. Then Mos had a serious problem: he aggravated a long-term back injury from a motorcycle crash. The awkward foot steering system on the boat had caused it. From inside the cabin I heard an ear-piercing scream and rushed out to see Mos twisted unnaturally on the seat.

It was plain that this was no bang on the wrist. He was in agony and could barely move. He explained that as he had been twisting his foot to turn the rudder, the boat had lurched and wrenched his back, aggravating the injury. The whole of his lower back had gone into spasm.

He really couldn't row now. I prepared to lift him back into the cabin so he could lie flat. That was not an easy process, as not only was he in agonizing pain, he was also covered from head to toe in skin cream. He was fanatical about skin care, which, although sensible as we generally rowed naked to reduce chafe, now transformed him into a man-sized eel. The farcical nature of wrestling my unhelpfully lubricated rowing partner into the cabin would have been hilarious were it not for the suffering it was putting him through.

Eventually I managed to get him inside, where he remained sedated with painkillers. After three days I pointed out to him that when the liquids I was regularly ditching overboard for him became solids, I would be summoning the safety yacht to remove him. At that point he emerged from the cabin ready for ablutions but still unable to row. We lost five days before he could row again. It was the vindication of our promise to each other that if one of us was incapacitated, the other would carry on. But despite my best efforts, we slipped back in the fleet.

As Mos recovered from that setback, one of his greatest strengths became apparent. Desperate to eke out every ounce of speed from the boat, he began adjusting the oar settings. I hadn't even been aware that there were settings. Apart from adjusting the lengths of the oars, principally so they didn't cross and trap your fingers, I thought the positions were fixed.

No, he assured me, the boat is getting lighter so we're higher out of the water. I can change the angle of the blades so it makes us more efficient and faster. I wasn't convinced, but I let him get on with it. When he'd finished adding washers to the gates and adjusting angles, I tried them out. The difference was remarkable: the speed improved almost immediately, and the effort to make that speed was reduced. He knew his stuff, and for the first time I recognized the value of technical rowing knowledge on an ocean rowing boat.

Those regular adjustments continued as Mos recovered and we fought to make up the ground we'd lost. One moonlit night, after his latest tweak to the rowing setup, I found myself rowing in the face of those big following seas generated by the unusually strong trade winds. Robbie Williams, who, despite being our only resident artist had not yet lost his appeal, was blasting out of the deck speakers for the umpteenth time. The rowing was effortless, and the speed was fantastic. Mos had set the boat up perfectly. We were storming toward the rest of the fleet and the finish line. Everything was great.

Then in the moonlight I saw a wave rear up that dwarfed the others around me. It was at least forty feet high, roaring toward the boat, and it was breaking. Desperately I twisted the footplate on the rudder to bring our stern into the face of the onrushing monster. Nothing happened. Not only did the stern not turn into the face of the wave to prevent a capsize, the boat began to go beam (sideways) on to it, the worst possible position.

The last thing I remember was *Charmed Life* heeled over on her side, marooned at the base of that gigantic wave as it reached us. I was looking directly up the length of my right oar toward where the stars had now been replaced by a mountain of water about to crash down on me.

Time froze, and for what must have been only a couple of seconds I remember sitting bracing myself as everything seemed to go silent.

Nothing happened while time froze. "I've gotten away with this," I thought.

Then there was a ferocious roar and the wave hit. I was smashed by a torrent of water that rolled the boat over and spat me off the deck. I wasn't attached to the boat, and now found myself submerged, tumbling under water, separated from the boat at night in big seas.

I remember exactly what was going through my mind: "Not here. I'm not going to die here on the Atlantic. On a training run."

As soon as I surfaced, gasping for air, I realized I had to locate the boat immediately. If I got a wave length away from her in those seas, I might never see her again. Fortunately, when these monstrous waves swept through, they invariably left a lull directly behind them. I came up in that lull and a few seconds later could see *Charmed Life* about thirty yards away, upside down and slowly resurfacing. As soon as I saw her, I swam for all I was worth to get back. As I closed on her, she slowly began to self-right, water streaming from her gunwales as she steadily came around. The white navigation light emerged, still in place and, unbelievably, still on.

When I finally reached her, I pulled myself over the bulwarks and rolled onto the deck, relieved and breathless. My arrival was greeted by Robbie Williams blasting from the speakers at the top of his voice, "Let meee entertain you!'"

It was a surreal touch to a near-death experience.

Mos was trapped in the cabin and in shock. He'd been asleep when the wave hit and had been hurled around the cabin as the boat was submerged and rolled repeatedly under the impact. It took me five minutes to get him out of the cabin. Luckily he was uninjured but he didn't know where he was.

A few miles away and around the same time, *American Fire Atlantic Challenge*, the boat previously called *Atlantic Star* belonging to my American friends from 2001 Tom Mailhot and John Ziegler, was caught out by a similar monster wave. There was a female team on board this year, and they were not so lucky as we were. Their boat was totally flooded when they capsized, and it couldn't self-right. They found themselves clinging to the hull of the upturned boat, waiting for rescue.

When we heard their Mayday, we contacted the ship (the youth training ship *Stavros S Niavros*) that was going to their aid to give them information. We listened on the VHF radio as the rescue progressed through the night. Both Emily Kohl and Sarah Kessans, the new crew, were safely picked up. But it could easily have been very different for all of us that night.

One question I'm always asked about that event is "Why weren't you tied on?"

If it had been my boat, I almost certainly would have been. But on *Charmed Life* the tethering system on board attached around the waist, making rowing practically impossible. So I'd given up on it. I would normally have used a much more practical leash connection around the ankle.

In fact, since the violence of the capsizing was so great, I'm convinced that I would have been seriously injured and likely knocked out if I'd been tied to the boat. It might have cost me my life. There are no absolute solutions. As a result, although I've always set my boats up since with effective tether points all over, I've rarely tied on.

I'm not saying that's the right choice, but it's my choice. I was taught to sail by people before the health-and-safety culture dominated. The people I respected most behaved as though they belonged at sea whatever size boat they were on. They didn't live in terror of the sea. They respected it. It may be a romantic, outdated notion, but that's how I approach it. I make sure every safety aid possible is available in case I should need it, but I rely on none of those aids more than my own judgment and common sense.

Fourteen days after capsizing, Mos and I proudly rowed into Nelson's Dockyard in Antigua, having successfully crossed the Atlantic Ocean. Only one wooden rowing seat had survived the capsize, and no chafe-preventing woolen seat covers or padding remained, so it was an uncomfortable last couple of weeks. I still have the scars on my backside to prove it.

We arrived on February 5 after 61 days, 2 hours, and 5 minutes at sea. I believe we came sixth in the race, only to discover as soon as we stepped ashore that we'd been disqualified for starting late. Mos was furious. I just smiled and said to him, "Mate, we've just rowed across the Atlantic Ocean. It doesn't get better than that."

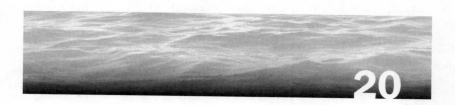

BACK TO JAPAN

WHEN I STEPPED ASHORE in Antigua, my main emotion was pride. Mos and I had crossed the Atlantic together. We had been relative strangers forty-eight hours before we'd started, and we'd come through the most challenging conditions successfully. It had been an incredible experience, and it had taught me an awful lot, not just about ocean rowing but also about myself. It had also shown me that I could function on a rowing boat as part of a team, something I'd doubted since Steve had left.

It also showed me that a two-man crew would have a lot greater chance of rowing under the Golden Gate Bridge from Japan than a solo would. Mos and I had rowed at every available moment as we made our way to Antigua, health permitting. That was how we'd managed to catch up with so much of the fleet: we had rowed two hours on, two hours off around the clock. That was the shift system that Steve and I had eventually settled on as the most efficient in 2001. I referred to it as always having someone at the coal face. As a solo rower, there's no way you can do that. You have to rest at some point. When you rest, you generally lose ground.

Returning to the North Pacific with a partner would mean there would always be someone at the coal face. That would be an essential weapon to counter the consistently awful conditions that would dominate that stretch of ocean.

The project was always about being the first to row under the Golden Gate Bridge, not just about my being the one to do it. So when all the evidence pointed to a pair making more sense than a solo, it was an easy decision to take a partner. My only problem now was, who was that partner going to be? Once more, luck, or fate, came to my aid.

A day or so after Mos and I arrived in Antigua, a solo rower named Chris Martin finished. I'd gotten to know Chris during the buildup to the race, and although we didn't know each other well, we got on fine. Chris was in his early twenties and a world-class flat-water rower, an immensely popular character in the race, and one of those guys you'd have to work hard to fall out with. He has a ready smile and is built like a middleweight boxer. Rowing an ocean was his idea of an adventure, just like mine. I suspected that, having done it once, he might be up for another go.

Almost everything on Chris's boat had broken during his crossing. He'd broken all of his oars, which unfortunately were the same unsuitable make as ours. Despite that, he'd managed to repair pretty much everything en route and still make landfall in Antigua. I had already been thinking he might be the perfect partner. Hearing that just confirmed it to me.

Much the way that Steve had proved a more natural engineer in terms of repairing gear on the 2001 crossing, Mos fulfilled the same role in 2005: in addition to constantly tweaking the rowing setup to gain more speed and efficiency, he just seemed to live to fix things. My maxim was: if it's not essential, do without. I certainly wouldn't spend time on something I felt didn't need to be fixed; I'd just find a way to work around not having it.

I recognized that as a weakness. I just didn't have that engineer's drive to solve every problem that crops up the moment it occurs.

That engineering capability in a rowing partner would be an enormous asset on a six-month voyage. Chris obviously had it, and his world-class rowing skills wouldn't hurt either.

I needed to ask Chris if he would be up for it, maybe even persuade him. I'll arrange to meet him at a bar, I thought. That should help.

As it turned out, Chris rang me first with exactly the same idea—meeting at a bar, not rowing the North Pacific. A few hours later we found ourselves discussing our Atlantic adventures over a steady flow of beer at the Antiguan dive bar the Mad Mongoose.

I knew Chris well enough to like him, which most people did as soon as they met him. I also knew him well enough to suspect that, like me, when he stepped off an ocean rowing boat he might be thinking he'd fancy a bit more of that. It was obvious within minutes that I was right. Despite a host of problems, including capsizing, he'd loved the experience. Whether that desire for a bit more stretched to the North Pacific, which was about as much more as you could get, remained to be seen.

I think I broached the subject by the second bottle of beer. Though flattered, he declined. He wavered over that decision during the third beer, and by the fourth we were starting to plan improvements to my boat. By the early hours of the morning, after a few more beers, we would both have happily pushed off from Japan right then and there. It looked as though I'd picked the right partner.

By the woozy light of the next day, Chris reviewed the decision. He needed some time to confirm that it was the right decision, not just one made in the euphoric wake of a successful Atlantic crossing. We both returned to the United Kingdom, and I began to adjust my plans.

Whatever Chris's final decision, I didn't have enough time to finish my boat and arrive in Japan by the end of April, which was now barely two weeks away. There was going to be a delay. I'd already learned the painful lesson of rushing to the start line less than fully prepared. I'd put back the attempt to allow myself time to complete the work properly and give Chris the time to confirm his decision one way or the other.

It didn't take him long to make up his mind. He was up for it. The Golden Gate Endeavour, the name of the project, became a two-man expedition. That was lucky for me, as I'd never have achieved anything without Chris on board.

My job with Woodvale was coming to an end, and with the delay of my return to Japan I needed to find a job in order to finish the work on my boat. Out of the blue, I was offered a position skippering a private yacht in Nigeria.

Initially, the contract was for six months. Ultimately, I would stay three years. It would prove to be the best decision of my life. It would provide the bulk of my funding for the return to the Pacific. And it introduced me to my wife.

It very nearly didn't happen, though. As I was walking to the interview for the job in Poole on the south coast of England, I received a phone call from the United States. It was Bill Wolbach, the producer from the US film production company Lantern Films who had attended the 2001 race. Bill and his son, Luke, had become great friends of mine and were eager to help with the planned documentary of the Pacific row.

"I hear you're thinking of going to Nigeria, Mick," Bill said.

"Yeah, maybe. I'm walking to the interview now."

"Why are you going there, man? It's a really dangerous place," Bill asked, obviously concerned.

"I need a job, and I need money for the Pacific."

"I'll sponsor you for the Pacific; whatever the amount you need, my company will sponsor you. You don't need to go to Nigeria."

It was an amazingly generous offer and typical of Bill. But I couldn't accept it. There wasn't nearly enough value for Bill's company in sponsoring me to justify the huge cost. Plus I was excited about the prospect of the job in West Africa. Forty-five minutes later I'd been offered the job and was making plans to move to Lagos.

GRACE

BILL WAS RIGHT. Lagos was a dangerous place, or at least it could be if you weren't careful. But it was also an incredibly exciting place. I loved it from the first minute I arrived.

Being an Englishman, I naturally moan about everything, particularly the weather. It's a national characteristic. Nigerians never moan. In three years of living and working in Lagos, I can't recall meeting one Nigerian who didn't think tomorrow would be a better day. The Nigerians, many living in abject poverty, still faced the world with a smile and a positive attitude. It's a lesson I've never forgotten.

It was a humbling and gratifying experience to live and work in such an environment. It was also as far removed from the normal routine of life in the private yachting world as you could wish. That's another reason I enjoyed it so much.

Once it was clear that the contract would be for three years and not just the six months originally mentioned, Chris and I settled on April 2009 as our date to arrive in Japan. That would allow me to finish my contract, as well as giving us plenty of time to get everything right. Though I didn't know at the time, it would also allow me time to get married.

There is an element of selfishness in taking on any ocean row-ing project. Having done four such voyages with a fifth in the pipe-line takes it to a whole new level. In my defense, I was aware of that and had tried as much as possible to avoid relationships that would always take second place to my rowing ambitions. I hadn't always succeeded, and I wasn't proud of it. I was nobody's idea of the ideal marriage partner. But one night, stranded on a street in Lagos hav-ing lost my driver, that was all about to change.

Lagos is a vast and bustling West African city, chaotic and teem-ing with millions of people, the overwhelming majority of whom live in poverty. With almost constant traffic gridlock, there is no easy way to get around. Locals use okadas, cheap and wildly dangerous motorcycle taxis. For a few pennies you jump on the back, take your life in your hands, and travel anywhere in the city.

In my privileged position, I had my own car and driver, Bernard, a gentle giant of a man. For an expatriate working in Lagos, a good driver is worth his weight in gold. Bernard was priceless.

In the chaos of Lagos, though, even the best drivers can have problems. So when I found myself stranded outside a shopping cen-ter when he was delayed and I had no way to contact him, I knew I was in trouble.

Most of the street crime I saw in Lagos involved people steal-ing to survive. Dignity and honesty were often the preserves of those of us with full bellies. I had nothing but sympathy for the people in that situation. That wouldn't, however, make me any less of a target for them as a white expatriate standing on the roadside in Lagos. I needed to sort out safe transport quickly.

The major problem was that if I picked the wrong taxi driver, I was as likely to be robbed by him as by any armed robber I might come across on the street. I walked to a line of locals at what appeared to be a taxi rank and asked the person who looked most trustworthy if she could help me find a safe cab. Coincidentally, she was also the most beautiful. She looked at me as if I were mad. Then I explained that I'd lost my driver and really didn't want to risk flagging a car down off the street.

Her name was Grace, which she told me when she eventually saw I wasn't actually mad, just stranded. She agreed to help. She spent the next ten minutes arranging what I hoped would be a relatively safe cab home for me. The moment I was about to board my carefully vetted taxi, Bernard pulled up. He'd been stuck in traffic, a not uncommon occurrence in Lagos.

Not thinking, I turned to get into my car, leaving Grace and a highly annoyed taxi driver who thought he'd lost his fare. What was I thinking? I'd put Grace in a really awkward situation. I turned around, walked over to the cab, and, calming the driver down, paid for the journey I no longer needed to take. Turning to Grace, I apologized for putting her to the trouble of interrogating most of the Lagos taxi-driving fraternity on my behalf for no reason. For once not thinking about rowing an ocean, I also asked her if she might want to grab something to eat sometime by way of thanks. She agreed, and our relationship grew from there.

I discovered that Grace had grown up in the north of the country in Kaduna and that as a young girl she and her Christian family had been burned out of their home. Muslim demonstrations had been used as the cover for a riot that ended with her and her sister and father sheltering in their home while Christian men and boys were murdered on the streets outside. During the night their home was set ablaze in an effort to flush them out into the open. They escaped through a window and over a fence and took shelter in a drainage ditch.

One of their Muslim neighbors came to find them, begging them to take refuge in her house before the rioters found them. The Muslim woman and her family took in five other Christian families and bravely stopped any of the rioters from entering their house, quoting the laws of the Koran to them as they hovered outside with machetes and scythes. Grace's father, along with the men and boys from the other families, hid on the roof. The rioters agreed not to enter but insisted that all the curtains be opened so they could see inside and check who was there. Grace and her sister had to watch as a murderous gang of machete-wielding murderers peered into every window, looking for the slightest excuse to burst in and massacre the terrified people sheltering inside.

She laughed nervously when recounting how in the middle of it all a toddler had innocently pointed up to the roof and said, "What's Daddy doing?" only to be cut off midsentence with a smack from his mum. They endured the situation for four days before daring to leave and make their escape south.

"I saw people outside being hacked to pieces and then burned while they were still alive," Grace told me sadly but matter-of-factly. "When we left, we were stepping over their bodies. I've never forgotten the smell."

It was hard to imagine how the smiling young woman I'd come to love, a person with boundless empathy for others and a remarkable zest for life, had remained so seemingly unscarred by those experiences. It was humbling to know her and reminded me how lucky I'd been in the lottery of birth that most of my challenges had been of my own choice.

Eighteen months after our first encounter, two weeks before I left Nigeria for Japan, we were married.

FINDING CAUSES

I MET ANOTHER remarkable woman while I was in West Africa. Her name is Theresa Laja Adedoyin. The daughters of my boss Femi Otedola, organized a spectacular fund-raising event for a clinic that Theresa had founded. I was invited and became fascinated by Theresa's story.

She'd had a serious motorcycle accident while riding as a passenger on one of those Okada taxis. Like many Nigerians, Theresa is a staunchly religious woman. Finding herself in hospital on the verge of losing her leg, she prayed to God. She told Him that if He would allow her to keep her leg, she'd devote the rest of her life to His work.

She eventually walked out of hospital and kept her promise in the most spectacular fashion: she set up Hearts of Gold Children Hospice, the first and only children's clinic in Nigeria, which takes in handicapped and sick children and babies abandoned on the streets of Lagos.

Grace and I visited one Christmas Eve to see Theresa and take some small gifts for the children. It remains one of the most memorable Christmas Eves I've ever had. The kids, at least those not too restricted by their disabilities, were having the time of their lives. They were obviously happy and secure in their surroundings. It was a wonderful and humbling experience. Theresa is as close to a saint as I suspect I'll ever meet.

The clinic was a three-room bungalow housing forty-six children with a variety of mental and physical disabilities. Most shockingly of all to me, they included thalidomide victims. Apparently, drugs containing thalidomide are still easily available from the unregulated pharmacies in Nigeria, though long since banned in the developed world.

One tiny newborn baby had arrived the night before Grace and I visited. She'd been found by the police dumped in a trash bin. They'd brought her to Theresa, the only person they thought could help. She was the most beautiful little girl, but unfortunately she'd been born with only one arm. Without intervention, that would likely have condemned her to a miserable, lonely death just a few hours after entering the world. It was beyond my comprehension how that could happen.

Every one of the forty-six children in the clinic had a heartbreaking story. The shocking thing was that if it hadn't been for Theresa and her staff, most if not all of them would not have been alive to tell it.

All of my rowing projects had been run with the goal of raising money for charity. I'd quickly become disillusioned with the soulless and sometimes cynical corporate nature of the larger charitable organizations. As a result, I'd been raising funds for Hamilton Lodge School for Deaf in Brighton.

Though they were a world apart, I recognized exactly the same qualities in the people working at Hearts of Gold as in those at Hamilton Lodge. They cared about what they did, their work mattered to them, and it shone through in their actions. It also shone through in the effect it had on the kids.

Anyone attending the annual Christmas pantomime, that peculiarly British mix of fairy tale, pop culture, and general nonsense, at

Hamilton Lodge, put on by the students, would see from the level of creativity, hard work, and energy that the kids loved their environment.

In a different way, Hearts of Gold created exactly the same environment for its kids. Theresa ran the place as efficiently as any sergeant major I've ever known. She had to. There were so many children dealing with so many different disabilities in such a limited space that it would have descended into chaos if it hadn't been run like a military organization.

There were, however, only smiling faces among the children living there, all of whom obviously adored Theresa. It was humbling to see those kids, despite everything they'd had to cope with in their young lives, so happy and content in the loving, secure home Theresa and her staff had created for them.

For my next Pacific project, I decided that any money raised would be divided between those two remarkable organizations.

JAPAN AT LAST

CHRIS AND I ARRIVED in Tokyo at the end of April 2009. Neil Kent, an old friend from Boston who'd been a constant supporter of all my rowing projects, came with us. Neil, an electrician by trade, had been in Japan to help me on both of my previous Pacific-crossing attempts. He'd gone to school with my brother, Steve, and I'd known him since I was ten years old. My parents considered him another son. Neil was the one person who was as certain as I was that one day I would reach San Francisco. Either that, or maybe he just liked visiting Japan.

The weather in Choshi was glorious. We hoped it would be a good omen for the future. It wasn't. Our boat was due to arrive in a few days, and our departure date was getting ever closer. The pressure for both Chris and me was naturally increasing, as it was for our loved ones back home.

Choshi was like a second home to me by this, my third visit. It was Chris's first. It can only have been daunting for him. One look at the rugged coastline would have given him a good indication of the ferocious seas this part of the world generated. If that wasn't a clear enough sign, just along the road from the marina, on a small hill, stands a monument to the scores of Choshi fisherman lost to the

Pacific. Our focus began to narrow, and we tuned in to the scale of the challenge that lay ahead.

The first thing I'd done when I'd originally decided to row across the North Pacific was visit Tim Welford and Dom Mee to get as much advice as possible after their unsuccessful row. They'd offered a wealth of useful practical and navigational information, but the one thing that always stayed with me was Dom's words as I was leaving: "Be careful out there. If you get it wrong, that place will kill you."

That's sound advice for mariners anywhere, but particularly appropriate for that vast, hostile stretch of water. It's the one piece of advice I've offered to everyone since who's asked me about rowing the North Pacific. That and "Don't go."

A couple of days after our arrival in Choshi, our rowing boat safely navigated her way through the sea of customs red tape and arrived in town on the back of a truck. With Neil's help, Chris and I got to work putting her back together, unpacking her, and checking all the systems.

Around the same time, we received a surprise visitor. Mos Morris, my erstwhile Atlantic rowing partner, decided to fly out to wish us well. It was great to see him, and his visit helped take our minds off the task at hand. Karaoke became a nightly pastime, and the tension lifted. I knew from experience that sitting in a hotel room endlessly looking at weather forecasts, thinking constantly about departure, was soul-destroying. That wasn't going to happen with Mos around. He was a walking party.

A few days later and after much activity, our boat was ready to go, as were we. We lowered her into the water and secured her. Now all we were waiting for was the precious weather window that would allow us twenty-four hours of favorable rowing conditions to escape the treacherous Japanese coastline.

I'd linked up with a US weather router, Lee Bruce, who runs Oceanmet, a global adventure meteorology service providing custom weather forecasts and premium weather routing for superyachts, ocean rowers, adventurers, and expeditions, for all of my trips on the Pacific. Lee was great at his job and became a great friend, although his manner of passing on information took a little getting used to. With Lee it was always the worst-case scenario. That is completely understandable, because especially on a small boat that's what you should be working from. The trouble was that on the North Pacific the worst-case scenario was often catastrophic. That meant that any forecast with an element of bad weather, as delivered by Lee, would be terrifying.

At the start of May, Lee informed us that a typhoon was heading our way. Although that would mean we couldn't leave before it arrived, after it passed the winds would drop and give us a window. We'd be leaving in heavy rain and facing a big swell, but the conditions would steadily improve and the wind would be with us. I knew only too well that we would have to take the first opportunity we were given, and this was it. There were never going to be perfect conditions to leave in.

Depending on the speed of the passage of the typhoon, we were looking at May 8 to start. We didn't have long, and the process for departure was complicated. A full inspection of the boat by the Japan Coast Guard was required, along with a meeting to confirm the passage plan and gain its authorization to depart.

Then we had to travel to the immigration offices to have our passports stamped for departure and clear customs. That was almost a two-hour drive from where we were staying. More awkwardly, once the passport was stamped you had to leave the country within twenty-four hours, meaning that any change in the weather would require the whole process to be repeated.

We were fortunate that we found a bottomless well of support from Choshi Yacht club and its members, particularly Kaz Ebata. He worked in the local mayor's office and was in his early sixties. He had helped Tim and Dom with their project and had been kind enough to provide me with the same support when I'd first arrived in 2003.

He'd been slightly alarmed to see me and just one friend turn up, but he'd steadfastly acted as our translator and fixer each time I returned to Choshi. It was no different in 2009. Kas was a constant and invaluable help to us and became a good friend, one of many we made in Choshi.

He drove us to the immigration and customs offices, where we had to be seen in person and get our passport stamps, and he even negotiated a couple of days' flexibility on our departure date when he explained the weather restrictions and the nature of our project to the officials. We'd have been lost without him.

Mos had to return to the United Kingdom before we left, so we waved him good-bye after a final bout of karaoke and prepared ourselves for the typhoon that we hoped would bring our weather window.

May 8 was a Friday. Right on cue, the storm blew through the day before. It gave everyone, including us, a small taste of the coming typhoon season. The morning of the eighth, the typhoon was still in full force, though weakening, and the town was drenched by constant downpours. Our projected window was in early afternoon. At 1 p.m., there was no sign of it arriving.

This window was crucial because the first of many challenges when we left Choshi would be safely crossing the busy lines of shipping transiting up and down the Japanese coast. There were two bands of shipping lanes, one inshore and the other miles offshore. Each had two lanes of traffic going in opposite directions.

The Coast Guard had sent a small patrol vessel to escort us through the inshore lanes, but it was keen for us to leave in daylight so as to not be transiting them at night. The officials told us there had been something like thirty-five collisions in those channels over the last few years. They didn't want another one.

As the clock ticked, we were on the verge of calling off the departure. It was getting too late in the day, and we'd have little light left. Then, just after 1 p.m., the wind finally began to die away to a level we could realistically cope with and changed to a direction that wouldn't halt our progress.

The decision was made. We'd leave at 2:30. It was still pouring rain, but the wind had almost died.

We shook hands with Neil and Kas and pushed off into the North Pacific. We were on our way.

THE BLACK CURRENT

ONE OF THE KEY aspects of rowing the North Pacific is escaping from the Japanese coast in one piece. The best way to ensure that is to row directly east for all you're worth from Choshi and embed yourself in one of the strongest currents in the world: the Kuroshio.

The Kuroshio, or Black Current, is a huge, powerful stream of warm water that sweeps up from the Philippines and flows past the coast of Japan. Just north of Choshi it arcs east to the open ocean and, like a serpent, snakes out for more than six hundred miles into the Pacific directly east of Japan.

It's a magic carpet ride for an ocean rowing boat, as it can move at up to 7 knots in places. If you can embed yourself in that current and stay there, you will have a six- or seven-hundred-mile free push out into the Pacific. That gives you crucial miles between you and the early-season typhoons and storms that regularly sweep up the east coast of Japan.

Of course, getting into the current is easier said than done. First you have to find it; then you have to stay in it. Every bend in the current and every storm brings the prospect of being thrown out, and once you're out, it can be impossible to get back in. There's also the risk of getting caught in one of the many eddies that break off from the main flow and sweep you around over hundreds of miles, back to where you started. That can eat up precious days, adding potentially hundreds of miles to the journey and effectively ending a voyage before it even starts. The ride on the Kuroshio might be free, but it's not easy.

The secret to locating it is simple: temperature. The water is about 16 degrees Centigrade (about 60 degrees Fahrenheit) when you leave Choshi. In the heart of the Kuroshio, it can be 23 degrees C. or more. On my first trip I took the thermometer from my parents' pub cellar to test the water temperature. (If anybody from Boston is reading this, that's probably why the bitter was warm that summer.) Our new boat, *Bo*, had a sensor built into her hull with a readout on deck. *Bo* was short for Bojangles, from the famous Sammy Davis, Jr., song "Mr. Bojangles." I'd chosen the name because it reminded me of growing up in my parents' pubs. Songs like that were the sound track of my childhood. I'd had a fantastic childhood, and I wanted that connection to good memories. It also gave *Bo* a personality. It's hugely important to treat your boat as another member of the crew and for the boat to have her own identity, and the right name is crucial in that process. You've got to care about her and look after her; that way, you believe, she'll care about and look after you. Obviously we had to change the name slightly from the song, as all boats are female, so we dropped the "Mr." and christened her *Bojangles*, which soon became the more affectionate *Bo*. It worked; even Chris, who hadn't had the benefit of a Rat Pack sound track to his childhood, grew attached to *Bo*, and she returned the favor and protected us both.

The Kuroshio can be situated anywhere from sixteen to forty miles off Choshi, and its location fluctuates. That's why you need that twenty-four-hour window to make sure you can reach it. According to the satellite readouts, the current was around twenty miles out when we left, so reasonably close. Once we'd safely navigated through the shipping lanes, we watched with glee as very slowly the water temperature readout began to increase.

We'd reached the outer edge of the current. Now all we had to do was row deeper into the middle, and we would be safely embedded. Even when the storms kicked in from the east, which they undoubtedly would, by using our parachute anchor we could hook ourselves into the current and it would drag us through any adverse winds. Remember, this time we weren't racing anybody. We just needed to make it across.

On my previous solo row, embedded in the Kuroshio, I'd covered more than 120 miles in a twenty-four-hour period. That was apparently a record for a solo rower at the time. The last ten hours of that time, I'd been locked in my cabin drinking tea from my flask with a tropical storm raging outside. My para anchor was deployed from the stern, and the Kuroshio was dragging my boat backward through the storm at five knots an hour. It wasn't comfortable, but it was effective.

As Chris and I settled into our first night's rowing on the North Pacific, we considered our start a huge success. We'd safely exited Choshi on the back of a typhoon, traversed the shipping lanes with no problems, and now here we were rowing into the heart of the Kuroshio. Everything was going exactly according to plan, our morale was high, and we were having a ball.

But the Pacific still had a terrifying welcome in store for us that would almost end our voyage before it had begun.

We'd both rowed out of Choshi, but once the small fleet of boats full of well-wishers, including our friend the increasingly green-looking Neil Kent, had returned to port, we reverted to the single rowing position, which we intended to use for the vast majority of the voyage. We planned to row two hours on, two hours off, twenty-four hours a day, whenever possible. It was the routine that had worked so well on the Atlantic for me in the past.

The lack of sleep was painful, but with two hours rowing you can sustain the pace for the whole shift. You can't consistently keep up the pace for three hours or more. If you want to sleep more, you're going to give up rowing efficiency and speed. We'd catch up on sleep when we reached California. We were here to row.

As we settled in to the night shifts, things could not have been going better. Then on my off shift I got a shout from Chris. He'd seen a light. "Several lights!" he shouted.

I'd told Chris when we were preparing to set off to give me a shout if he saw any lights at all. Apart from his Atlantic crossing, Chris had no seagoing experience; I was a professional sailor, so I could identify what the lights belonged to and, more important, assess if there was a likely risk of collision. When Chris called, I presumed he'd spotted a passing ship's navigation lights.

When I came out on deck, Chris pointed over his shoulder. "Look at that," he said.

The horizon was awash with navigation lights, and judging by the type of lights on display, they were a fleet of fishing boats. To this day, I've never seen so many in such close proximity at sea. I counted fifty boats.

"What are they?" Chris asked.

"Fishing boats, mate. Loads of 'em."

The warm waters of the Kuroshio were a prime fishing location. We joked that they must be replacing all the sushi we'd consumed during our stay in Japan. There wasn't much we could do. They were still a few miles away from us. And they stretched along a distance of at least two miles, so we could hardly row round them.

"Just keep your eye on them, mate. Hopefully they'll head off in another direction before we get too close," I said before returning inside. "Give me a shout if they start to get much closer."

We shadowed that enormous fishing fleet for the next few hours. Nothing much changed. They didn't seem to be heading off in a different direction, but they weren't getting any closer, either. Later that night, when I was sleeping, all that suddenly changed. I woke to the long booming blast of a ship's horn, obviously very close. I jumped out on deck. There was a large trawler six or seven hundred yards off our port side, presumably the boat that had sounded her horn. Chris sat in the rowing position, looking at me.

"I was just going to give you a shout, mate. Look!" He gestured behind him with his thumb.

The fleet of fishing boats was now almost on top of us, and at that distance I could make out exactly what they were. As well as dozens of trawlers, there were huge mother ships, several of them ablaze with deck lights and busy unloading trawlers rafted up either side with huge cranes. The trawlers had small tugs attached to them, pulling at right angles to keep them from smashing into the side of the mother ship in the increasingly choppy seas.

Chris was pointing to one of the mother ships, directly ahead of us. It had a trawler on either side and a warp line stretching out at right angles at least two hundred yards, with a tug on the end heaving the trawlers off the mother ship. It was an obstacle seven hundred yards across blocking our path.

The thick warp line the tug was attached to was scything up and down like a guillotine. If we crossed between the tugs and the trawler, it would smash our boat to pieces and us with it. The trawler on our port side had obviously seen the growing threat and had blasted his horn to warn us. It wasn't a moment too soon. If ever there was a time to have a world-class rower on the oars, this was it.

The wind was blustery and on our port beam. There was a big swell. It wasn't easy rowing, but at least the wind direction gave us a chance to get around that huge and potentially deadly obstruction.

"Chris, turn to starboard and row like fuck, mate. We have to get around that right-hand tug!"

It was the farthest away, but it was our only option. If we'd tried to get around the left-hand tug, which we were closest to, the wind would have steadily blown us onto it or, even worse, through the deadly warp line that was crashing up and down in the sea in front of us. Chris dug in and heaved our fully laden one-ton rowing boat on the new course. We were within a hundred yards of the stern of the mother ship as we crossed behind it.

Our boat was rising and falling in six-foot waves with the ominous sight of the thick warp from the right-hand tug crashing in and out of the sea just off our port (left) side. We could hear the drone of the trawler's machinery over the roar of the waves. All of the boats were lit up with deck lights, and we could hear the crews shouting, presumably at us. A couple of the boats blew their horns, also no doubt for our benefit. The loud blasts only added to the tension.

We were already doing everything we could to escape the situation. The crew on the tug could see our dilemma, but if they changed their position or released the warp, it would cause the trawler to smash against the side of the mother ship. There was nothing they could do to help.

If I'd been at the oars, I doubt we'd have made it. I wasn't a powerful enough rower. Chris had an extra gear and went into overdrive. I stood in front of the cabin, emergency flare in hand, as slowly, and with a Herculean effort, Chris dragged *Bo* narrowly past first the mother ship and trawlers and then finally the right-hand tug.

We were no more than thirty yards ahead of its bow as we cleared her. It had taken Chris something like forty nerve-wracking minutes to haul us free of what would have been a catastrophic and potentially lethal end to our voyage. It had felt like forty hours to me, and I hadn't rowed a stroke. I couldn't imagine how Chris felt.

When we were finally past the bulk of the fishing fleet, Chris looked at me and smiled wanly. "It's not going to be like this all the way, is it, Mick?"

"I bloody well hope not, mate!" I replied.

A PACIFIC STORM

WE DIDN'T have to wait long for the next challenge. It came in the shape of our first Pacific storm.

Thanks to Lee's constant weather updates, on the third night we were fully expecting the storm, which emerged menacingly over the horizon. Bursts of heavy rain heralded the approach of the front, distant cracks of thunder and streaks of lightening signaled the main event that was to follow. We were racing along in the Kuroshio at that point, gobbling up the miles. We'd successfully negotiated the first turn of the current without losing it and we were flying, heading almost due south to the next turn east.

The current's path was more pronounced in 2009 than it had been in 2004. On my earlier solo row, the Kuroshio had snaked east in a long, lazy, flowing pattern. This year it flowed more like a snake poised to strike, its bends much steeper and closer together as it turned sharply from north to south and south to north on its slow easterly progress.

With the speed of the Kuroshio and our rowing efforts combined, we were powering along at 8 or 9 knots at times, four times the average we would normally hope to maintain.

Much as on the Atlantic, the plan was to row the boat as long as we possibly could when storms began to form because every mile gained was crucial. We weren't racing other boats on the Pacific, but we were racing winter, a much deadlier opponent.

At the beginning, we were just getting soaking wet with the downpours. The wind, although increasing, was from a helpful direction, at least in terms of the path of the current. *Bo* was already demonstrating what a great sea boat she was. As Chris took over for his shift at midnight with the thunder and lightning increasingly close, he asked me when he should call it a day.

"As soon as you think it's picking up too much, mate. Or that stuff"—I pointed toward the thunder and lightning—"starts to get too close." I trusted his judgment.

I retired to the cabin and quickly fell into an exhausted sleep. I'd expected Chris to join me within the hour. When my alarm woke me at the next watch change, I was surprised he hadn't. From the motion of the boat, I could tell the seas had increased, and there were flashes of lightning and rumbles of thunder obviously much closer than before. Why hadn't he come in yet?

I stuck my head out the hatch. Chris was on the oars, wrestling gamely against the now-formidable waves rushing by. As well as the size of the sea, I instantly felt the electricity in the air. In the darkness Chris's hair seemed to be standing on end as he looked toward me wide-eyed, like a deer caught in headlights.

"Should I come in now, Mick?" he shouted over the roar of the waves.

"Yes, mate," I replied. "I think you'd better. I think you should have probably come in about an hour ago," I added, laughing.

He threw out the drogue on a long line from the stern. That would help keep the stern of the boat facing into the wind and the building sea, but it wouldn't kill our boat speed as the para anchor would. The wind was blowing us in the right direction, directly along the course of the Kuroshio. All we wanted to do was avoid capsizing. The drogue would do that job perfectly well.

Just ahead of a massive downpour accompanied by volleys of thunder and lightning, seemingly right on top of us, Chris crawled into the cabin next to me. I picked up the camera to quickly film his reaction and catch some of the increasingly dramatic weather outside.

"What's the reason we're doing this again?" he asked, laughing.

"Nobody's ever done it before, mate," I answered.

Those two lines became our mantra whenever the Pacific was doing its best to defeat us. We said it a lot over the next six and a half months.

Outside, the electrical storm continued to roll over us, punctuated by violent flashes of illumination and terrifying claps of thunder. Eventually, despite the turmoil surrounding us, exhaustion took over and we both fell asleep, happy to accept the free miles as we raced along the face of the storm deep in the flow of the Kuroshio current.

The first three days had provided quite a welcome to our Pacific adventure. Neither of us was in any doubt about the size of the task that lay ahead of us

As the storm passed the next day, we settled back into the routine we expected to follow for the rest of the voyage. We each put in a relentless two hours on, two hours off, rowing around the clock. We had to be cautious in the Kuroshio, though, because it was so easy to row out of it and so hard to find afterward.

As we progressed, I don't think Chris really grasped the importance of how reliably the current was pushing us away from Japan. It didn't help that the flow was so pronounced as we headed south on the second southerly loop of the current that we were actually losing miles toward San Francisco, at least in the short term.

Chris had put the destination "San Francisco" into the GPS. I'd deliberately left it off. I knew we had months of fighting the conditions on the Pacific ahead of us, which would include many miles going backward. Staring at a steadily increasing number when that happened wasn't going to help morale.

I explained to Chris that my approach was to take the trip in small bites. We'd set a short-term goal, then tick it off as we cracked it. Reaching one goal at a time, one day we'd wake up looking at the Golden Gate Bridge. It was a psychological approach I'd developed during my solo trip as I discovered the crushing frustrations of making ground on the Pacific.

"Our goal right now, mate, is to maximize the use of the Kuroshio," I told Chris. "That's all that matters. Take the trip one small bite at a time. Forget about San Francisco, we can worry about that later."

Chris wasn't convinced. He was keen to have the miles to San Francisco on display. He wanted to see the big picture. Frustratingly, that meant that as we powered down the southern flow of the Black Current for the second time, the miles-to-go number actually started to increase.

"We've cracked over a hundred miles today, mate," I said at one point. Which was great progress.

"Yeah, but we're three miles farther away from San Francisco," he replied dejectedly.

He saw miles to go as the only important metric. In truth, the only important goal was navigating the current successfully. The key at that stage was to stay in the Kuroshio, which would ultimately take us east, however haphazardly. This was my third time navigating it, but Chris started to lose faith. He wanted to head directly east. The miles to San Francisco steadily increasing on the display didn't help his frame of mind.

Around that time there was also a threat that we could be caught in an eddy heading back to Japan as the current began its next turn east. That sowed a seed of doubt in my mind. Combined with Chris's constant concerns about mileage and despite my better instincts, I agreed that we should head out of the current and basically cut the corner where the Kuroshio turned to head north again.

As we exited the express conveyor belt of the Kuroshio, the water temperature dropped and the boat's speed crashed. We were now rowing at an average of little more than 2 knots, or a third of our previous speed. Every yard gained from that point on would be down to us; there'd be no more free miles unless we found the current again.

Much more worryingly for me, if the wind turned against us, we'd be static or slowly going back on the para anchor, no longer gaining ground from the current, and we'd be sitting ducks for the next typhoon.

The moment we left the current behind, it was obvious it was the wrong decision. I should have known better, but I'd allowed the worry of being swept back to Japan in the eddy and Chris's lack of faith in the current to cloud my judgment. Now we had to find the next stretch heading north before the weather turned.

It took us a nerve-wracking day and a half of slow progress, but before the weather had a chance to add to our woes we'd dragged ourselves back into the northern flow of the Kuroshio and were safely back on our magic carpet ride away from Typhoon Alley. The Black Current was taking a particularly meandering path that year, but ultimately it would get us to where we needed to be. I'd made a mistake deciding to leave it, but luckily, we'd gotten away with it.

WHERE THERE'S SMOKE

AS MUCH AS the Kuroshio was a key factor in our planning, in the overall scheme of things it made up only a very small part of the voyage. A little over six hundred miles from the coast of Japan, it began to weaken and eventually disappeared. Our free ride east was finished. Every mile now would be hard earned, some of them repeatedly.

We were settling into the routine well. Our boat was performing fantastically, and, although exhausting, the rowing was proving manageable. We had made great progress. That would slow now with the free miles of the current behind us, but we'd been expecting that and were now both relishing the next challenge.

Chris's excellence as an engineer soon came into play, when, having emerged from some bad weather, I noticed our batteries weren't charging. We had a battery management system in the cabin that displayed all the data. For some reason, the display showed that there was no longer any charge coming from the solar panels.

We soon discovered that one of the electrical joint boxes on the cabin roof had been partially corroded by salt water. As a result, it looked as though we'd lose the output from several solar panels. That would have proved to be a major problem. Chris got to work on a solution. Two hours later the problem was solved and *Bo*'s batteries were back on charge again. Chris had managed to bypass the electrical fault and get all the panels on line again. We'd not lost a yard's progress, as I'd continued rowing throughout the repair. The partnership was working exactly as we'd both hoped.

That would not prove to be our last electrical problem on board. The next one, however, very nearly proved fatal.

It was several weeks later in the voyage. I was rowing. Chris was off watch and asleep in the cabin. It was an overcast, gray, misty day. In a wallowing lazy sea, with little wind, rowing was hard and slow. We were both in a permanent state of exhaustion by now with the punishing rowing routine we were employing. So when I noticed the compass, which was fitted above the cabin hatch, spinning, my first reaction was that I was hallucinating.

When the dial kept swinging wildly one way, then the other, my next, utterly bizarre, thought was "Alien abduction."

It didn't stop, and I wasn't beamed up to a UFO. I stared at the compass, trying to come up with a rational explanation. Suddenly the compass seemed to go hazy. What the hell was going on? Then I realized that the hatch below it was not sealed and there was a slight gap to let air into the cabin. Heat, or possibly smoke, was pouring out of the hatch!

I jumped from the rowing position and ripped the hatch open. Inside, the cabin was full of thick black smoke. Chris was in his sleeping bag, motionless.

"Chris!" I screamed. "We've got an electrical fire!" I shook him as hard as I could. He mumbled and started to wake, then jumped up.

"What the—?"

"Turn off the power, it's got to be the electrics."

Chris pulled open the locker beneath him and switched off the main power supply switch,. shutting off the flow of power to whatever was on fire. The cabin was full of toxic fumes. Chris opened the back hatch to let them escape. He was clearly still disoriented but thankfully conscious.

We looked around the cabin to see what had caught fire. We opened the main control panel, then the deck lockers. We looked everywhere but couldn't find anything. I was sitting on the deck outside with the hatch open looking in at Chris when I saw something over his shoulder: a vivid scorch mark around one of the bolts holding a solar panel in place.

"Look at that, Chris," I said.

It was obviously the cause of the smoke. The carbon fiber hull had been smoldering, not actually catching fire but producing loads of highly toxic black smoke. Thank God the hatch hadn't been completely shut.

We discovered that the solar panel on the outside of the cabin, to which the bolt was attached, had cracked. That crack had allowed the charge from the panel to short to the bolt. Unfortunately, the bolt, although it had been sealed when fitted, had somehow made contact with the carbon fiber hull, which was conductive. Inside the systems control box on the other side of the cabin there was one tiny screw on the negative (earth) electrical bar that hadn't been totally sealed and was screwed into the hull.

That mind-boggling series of coincidences had created a circuit for the charge from the broken solar panel to follow. That had electrified the hull; hence the spinning magnetic compass. Much more seriously, the heat generated around the bolt had caused the carbon fiber to smolder, creating the toxic fumes. Luckily, we'd reacted quickly enough to avoid the boat fully catching fire.

It had been an incredibly narrow escape. If the hatch had been sealed shut, as it usually was, I wouldn't have seen the smoke and Chris would have been fast asleep in the fume-filled cabin. It wasn't lost on us both, as we cleared up the mess from the fire, that by that stage we'd ridden out any number of storms sleeping in the cabin together. If the fault had developed then, we'd both have died in our sleep.

SEAMOUNTS

AS DAYS TURNED INTO WEEKS and weeks began to turn into months, we found ourselves approaching the next major navigational hazard, a huge range of undersea mountains, called seamounts, basically the extension of the Hawaiian Island chain beneath the sea, some submerged by as little as eleven feet.

Our broad plan had been to hold a southerly course, which would increase the distance we'd have to row but leave us in a better position to make it into San Francisco when we ultimately reached the US coast. I'd discovered on my aborted solo row that the Pacific currents and to a far greater degree the winds consistently force you north, and as much as that might still allow a west coast US finish, it would not be in San Francisco.

The seamounts were farther south than we had planned to venture. We were making good progress and were two weeks away from them. The forecast consistently promised weather that would allow us to pass safely north of them. But, although forecast, the southerly or southwesterly winds never arrived.

To complicate matters further, we found ourselves in a current taking us directly east. It was helpful in terms of making miles toward the United States but shortened our time frame to escape north and avoid the seamounts. We'd later discover that the easterly current we found ourselves in was the top of a huge circular eddy hundreds of miles across that swept east and then south directly down the inside of the seamounts. In fact, it appeared to be created by them. If we didn't escape north, it would take us with it.

As the miles ticked down toward the seamounts, the wind continued to defy the forecast and left us stranded in the current, which was ultimately dragging us to disaster. Navigating the seamounts, where the bottom of the ocean went from nearly four miles beneath us to just eleven feet deep in a few miles, would be fraught with danger. Any kind of serious weather, and the sea state would become deadly. The swell was higher than eleven feet on the Pacific even in fairly light conditions, in a storm we'd be smashed to pieces.

The countdown to that potential disaster continued for more than two weeks, until finally we were within forty-eight hours of reaching the top of the seamount range. Still in the current, we were making great progress east, but we needed to escape farther north immediately. We had one more weather forecast that promised some southerly wind. That was our last hope. It came, but too late.

There was something like a ten-hour window before the wind would come around to gale force from almost directly north. That would have left us at best just a few miles north of the submerged islands in the face of a northerly gale, which would then blow us straight down onto them.

We decided that the risk was too great and stayed in the current. Our only hope was that the current would sweep past the top of the seamounts and take us with it. That was unlikely, however. Everything pointed to the current being a huge eddy created by the island chain. We didn't have to wait long. As the window of escape north disappeared, our course began to slip south. The current was turning, taking us south down the leading face of the undersea islands.

As our course slowly changed, I started to work out the options. We'd done the right thing by not punching north at the last minute, which would have left us stranded in the face of the expected gale. But now we were heading south and potentially in a complete circle for hundreds of miles. There was an escape route about two hundred miles away, where the seamounts were not so close to the surface, but there was no guarantee that the weather would allow us to escape the current when we reached that point. It would also leave us way off our intended course.

As the gale approached, I pored over our chart. There was one other option, but it was not without risk. There was a narrow path through a group of seamounts just to the south of us. If we pushed out into the path, it would leave us more than twenty miles north of one seamount about twenty feet beneath the surface but just a mile or two south of the one submerged at just eleven feet. With the predicted force 8 northerly gale coming, that would effectively give us a twenty-mile safety margin and we could make our way between them. It might be enough.

The more I pondered the alternative, staying in the current for hundreds of miles in the hope of escaping south of the islands, the more I believed it was worth taking a calculated risk. I spoke to Chris about my thoughts. He was no more enthusiastic about navigating between those submerged mountain peaks than I was, but he shared my concern about heading so far south. We had very little time to make up our minds. We were steadily drifting south in the current and would need to row out of it soon if we were to make the gap. We would have to be free of the current before the forecast gale arrived, as that would end any rowing progress.

We made the decision and began to row due east. Several brutal shifts later, I was entering my second hour at the oars. We'd emerged from the current no more than twenty minutes earlier. It was easy to tell, as the course east became easier to maintain and the boat speed increased, we were no longer being dragged south, no longer in the current. The shallowest seamount was just two or three miles away from us, thankfully to the north, the direction from which the gale was predicted to blow.

The wind dropped away to nothing. A few minutes later, I felt a kiss of wind on my cheek approaching from the opposite direction. Within ten minutes, the wind was blowing consistently from the north-northeast strongly enough to make rowing impossible. I deployed the para anchor and hoped that we'd gained enough ground to stay out of the current. I suspected that we had managed to clear the current dragging us south by no more than a mile. If we hadn't, that would have been the end of our voyage. Such small margins would become a theme of our adventures on the North Pacific.

Within a couple of hours, the predicted gale arrived and, despite the para anchor, began to force the boat steadily south. It was a tense few hours on board but the twenty miles we had in hand above the seamount south of us proved sufficient to allow us to pass safely.

For the next four days we made our way between the submerged mountaintops hidden just below the sea, rowing for all we were worth when we could and hanging on to every mile gained on the para anchor when we couldn't. It was as tense an experience as hanging on to the Kuroshio had been, although this time potentially fatal.

If a major storm had come through, the seas would have been catastrophic. There would have been little chance of rescue, either, as large ships could not have safely navigated the area to come to our assistance.

Four days after we decided to exit the current to pick our way through that treacherous range of mountains just beneath the hull of our boat, we emerged unscathed on the other side of them. Relief was the biggest of understatements to describe our emotions. The calculated risk had paid off.

28

FEAR OF FOG

THAT TERRIFYING STRETCH of ocean had one more scare in store for us. At one point we'd noticed a fishing boat just a few miles away. No doubt the sudden rise in the ocean floor had thrown up an abundance of fish. As we emerged clear of the last seamount and night arrived, we found ourselves rowing in thick fog with visibility less than six feet.

On my solo voyage, fog had been a constant and terrifying hazard, sometimes for up to a week at time. Having to endure days of thick fog was the worst kind of mental torture, adding exponentially to the constant fear of collision. Our course this time was largely beneath the more northerly fog line, so as we found ourselves engulfed in it for the first time that night, it was a new experience. The one good thing was that we were in a stretch of water where there would almost certainly be no other ships, except for the fishing boat we'd seen earlier.

I woke to relieve Chris in the middle of the night. Dolly Parton, a favorite singer on our trip, was blasting out of the speakers. It made for an eerie, unnerving experience to come on deck with the boat blanketed in fog while Dolly belted out country songs. We couldn't see anything, and with Dolly belting out her classics we couldn't hear anything, either.

As Chris went back into the cabin, I asked him to turn off the music. Within a few minutes the slow rumble of a ship's engine could be heard somewhere in the wall of fog that surrounded us. It could have been five miles away or five hundred feet away; in the fog it was impossible to tell.

We had a new system on board, an automatic identifying system (AIS), which basically gave our coordinates to any passing ships and "painted" our picture on their radar. It had worked fantastically well up to that point, and the constant threat of collision that had dominated my previous voyage had been almost completely eliminated. But fishing boats tended not to carry the system or, if they did, didn't use it. We were in a substantial fog bank with a nearby fishing boat that was unlikely to see us electronically.

I called to Chris, and he came out on deck with pots and pans to bang and a spotlight. Our signal horn had given up the ghost some weeks earlier. It must have been the fishing boat we'd seen earlier in the day. The steady rumble of its engines continued to grow. Chris tried to call the ship on the VHF radio but got no response.

As I rowed, Chris stayed on deck, and we both tried to work out where the sound was coming from and how close the boat was. For the only time in the trip we put on life jackets. Any collision would have been sudden and catastrophic. We had to be prepared.

The ghostly encounter lasted for at least an hour, before the engine sounds finally began to diminish and we allowed ourselves to breathe a sigh of relief. It was impossible to tell, but I suspect we'd been within a hundred yards of the vessel during our fogbound encounter that night. The captain had never sounded his fog signal, so it's safe to assume that he had no idea we were there. Thousands of miles out in the Pacific, we had once again found ourselves only yards from disaster.

With the fog finally lifting and the threat of both the fishing boat and the seamounts behind us, our morale lifted considerably. But the improved shipboard mood was short lived.

Within twenty-four hours of leaving the fog bank behind us we rowed into what felt like molasses. It was another eddy, this one much weaker than the one we'd previously rowed out of, but it killed our boat speed. We were struggling to hold a course and make even one knot in the right direction. Even worse, every stroke felt as though the boat were filled with rocks. Every two-hour shift became purgatory.

After a couple of days, I remember taking over from Chris and finding that he was overjoyed. The boat speed had picked up, the rowing was becoming lighter again, and those GPS miles to San Francisco were going down.

"I think we've cracked it, Mick," he said.

Well, we'd cracked one side of the eddy. By the end of the day, we were back into the other side, the ocean had regained the consistency of liquid cement, and our boat speed was less than a knot. That eddy would prove to be the first of three, side by side, each one dozens of miles across. It took us more than two miserable, soul-destroying weeks to drag ourselves through them. I'd experienced similar setbacks on my solo trip. It was typical of the North Pacific and the definition of the challenge we faced.

Chris reached his lowest point during that ordeal. When he filed his blog update, he described it as "My own personal hell!"

Having experienced months of similar frustrations before, I'm ashamed to say that I had little sympathy for him. I should have had more compassion for my friend, as very shortly I would experience my own, very personal hell.

29

TERRIBLE NEWS

IT WAS JULY 9, the end of my 6 a.m. rowing shift, and Chris and I were handing over. It was baking hot, with light winds and consequently hard rowing. One of the joys of our trip was text messages from my brother, Steve, on the satellite phone. They were a constant morale booster for us.

Steve's messages generally concerned the full English breakfasts he'd recently enjoyed or the massive Sunday roasts, as well as regular updates on any Guinness consumed. They became a standing joke with us. As I was about to disappear into the cabin, Chris said, "Your brother hasn't sent any messages for a while, has he?"

I've no idea why, but when he said that an ominous feeling swept over me. I knew that something was wrong. I went into the cabin, pulled out the computer, and set up the Iridium satellite phone to download our email messages. I almost never did that, as it was very much Chris's part of ship.

Messages began to pour into my inbox. Principal among them was one from Steve with "Urgent!" in the subject line. My heart sank. I pressed on the message, and the most devastating words I'd ever read appeared before me: "Mick, ring home as soon as you can. Dad's had a setback. A serious one. He's got an infection and been rushed

193

into hospital. It's not over 'til the fat lady sings but it looks like we might lose him."

It was as if my stomach was being turned inside out and a ton of lead dropped on my shoulders at the same time. I was suspended somewhere between shock and disbelief. I disconnected the Iridium phone from the computer and called the family pub. It was late evening at home, July 8, a day earlier than us, as we'd yet to cross the International Date Line.

My brother answered. "I thought it would be you, Bruv," he said sadly. "Dad died ten minutes ago."

I was speechless and overcome with grief. I didn't know what to say or even how to feel. As grief threatened to overwhelm me, guilt was not far behind it. How could I be out here in the middle of nowhere when this happened?

Steve said immediately, "This was always going to be the worst day of our lives. It doesn't make it any different that you're out there. Just get this finished for the old man and get home."

I put the phone down and let the anguish of the moment sink in. Dad had been ill for some time, fighting an extremely rare type of lymphoma. But he'd seemed to be coming through it. Before I left he'd started a new treatment, and the early signs had been encouraging. I would never have left if I'd thought we were going to lose him. In fact, I know that subconsciously I believed that by going I would guarantee he'd be okay. He'd never die before I got back. He'd refuse to.

If I'd been on the moon, I'd have been no more remote from home and my family than I was then. The isolation overwhelmed me as the immensity of my loss engulfed me.

The hatch to the cabin was partially open to let some air circulate. Chris had placed a towel over the window to provide some shade in the cabin. It at least offered me some privacy as I buckled under my grief. As my two hours off watch steadily slipped by, I was consumed by one thought: "How am I going to tell Chris what's happened? How am I even going to be able to articulate it?" It's ludicrous thinking back on it, but in my despair and grief that was the only thing I was focused on.

As the time approached when I'd have to open the hatch, I rehearsed again and again in my head what I would say. I wouldn't break down. I wouldn't be weak. Above all, I wouldn't stop rowing. I clung to the fact that I had to row as the one point of stability in my otherwise crumbling world. It was five minutes to the hour. Time to relieve Chris.

I pushed the hatch open and looked out to where Chris sat working on the oars, oblivious to the news I'd received.

"Mate," I said without making eye contact and stumbling onto the deck, "I'm going to be a bit fucked up for a while. My dad has just died. Just let me row, and I'll be okay."

If I had said one more word, I'd have broken down for sure. Chris was in shock but instinctively knew what to do. He moved aside from the seat and let me take over in the rowing position. There were any number of times during our voyage across the Pacific when Chris excelled as a friend and a rowing partner, but never more so in the seconds that followed that stumbling declaration.

"Mate, I am so sorry," he said. "Look, whatever you want to do, just tell me and we'll do it. Anything you need, just tell me. I am so sorry, mate."

It was exactly the right thing to say at the right time, at least for me. I needed to be alone. Ridiculously, I was embarrassed at my own grief. Once again I was being stereotypically British and male, unable to give way to the most devastating emotion I'd ever felt in case it betrayed weakness. Chris knew me well enough to understand that and disappeared into the cabin. I remained at the oars alone and wept.

I missed only thirty minutes of rowing during the rest of that dreadful day, when Chris took over so I could ring my mum when she returned from the hospital.

"I wouldn't have left if I thought he was going to die, Mum," I kept repeating.

"Just get it finished for him, Son. That's what he would have wanted," she replied softly.

I knew Mum was right. That's exactly what Dad would have wanted, for me to carry on. I knew beyond any doubt that that was exactly what I should do. What I didn't know at that stage was if I could.

30

CORNED BEEF BALLS!

FOR A WHILE the rowing saved me. It held me together. By completely engrossing myself in the routine, which was relentlessly brutal, I could keep my grief and my increasing feelings of guilt at bay. I was too exhausted to think.

I wasn't sleeping during my two-hour naps. When I did sleep, I woke to the shocking realization of my dad's death. I was dreading the weather changing and finding myself on the sea anchor again, going nowhere. Without the structure of the two-hours-on, two-hours-off rowing to cling to, I would be completely overcome with grief.

Several days later I started to notice a trend in the weather. I contacted Lee, our weather guru. "I'm looking at the weather, Lee. Please don't tell me what I suspect is coming. I'm not sure I could cope with being stuck on the para anchor."

Unfortunately for me, a period on the sea anchor was exactly what was forecast. Lee reluctantly informed me that a week of unfavorable winds would be coming in the latter part of July. It felt like one more knife through my heart. I was sure I would go insane sitting on the sea anchor, drifting backward.

My world seemed to be steadily falling apart around me.

As the wind slowly changed direction and we deployed the parachute anchor, I dreaded the days of stalled progress. But, bizarrely, it turned out to be the best thing that could have happened.

With the rowing halted, at least for the time being, I was no longer driving myself into the ground with the relentless two-hour shifts at the oars and little or no sleep. I managed to get some sleep and began to feel stronger, and my thoughts were clearer.

As Chris and I settled in for another stint on the sea anchor, the date of my dad's funeral approached. I began to appreciate that I was in a rare situation for a son who'd lost a much-loved father. Isolated on the Pacific, I had nothing to think about except my dad, the life he'd given me, and the experiences we'd shared.

At home my family had the task of organizing the funeral, informing family and friends, and dealing with the undertaker and the endless red tape that surrounds a death. They would have little time for themselves and even less time to think about Dad. I was privileged in that I had nothing but time to remember him. That realization brought a feeling of gratitude combined with a wave of guilt at being absent, not for Dad but for them.

The hour of his funeral in England was nighttime for me and Chris out on the Pacific. I made myself a cup of hot chocolate and lay on the deck staring at a clear sky of endless stars. The wind, although still from the wrong direction and keeping us from making progress, was thankfully quite light. Chris had kindly offered to mark the event on the boat in any way I thought appropriate. All I wanted—no reflection on Chris—was to be alone with my thoughts. He disappeared into the cabin. I remained on deck.

For several hours I did nothing but lie there looking into the universe, thinking about the experiences we'd shared and all that he and Mum had done for my brother and me. None of the rowing adventures would have happened without their support. Memories passed through my brain like shooting stars. Skydiving in Italy on Dad's sixtieth birthday, a surprise he could possibly have done without. Seeing Dean Martin live at the London Palladium singing "Little Ole Wine Drinker Me." Watching Dad and Mum receive a standing ovation in the House of Blues in New Orleans jiving to "Johnny B. Goode."

Life is precious because it's finite. My brother had presciently said that dad's death would be the worst day of our lives. My stuck-at-sea situation afforded me a privilege few people are given in such circumstances: I got to spend those hours with my dad, no distractions, just him and me for one last time. I remembered a rich, full life well lived. The guilt of not being there for a man who'd always been there for me was eased by the understanding that we had indeed made the most of the time we'd had together. Not everyone can say that.

There's no choice about dying. It's going to happen to all of us. The choice comes in how you live. My dad had lived well and had made some good choices. Recognizing that helped.

Back home in Boston, hundreds of people packed the funeral service and the parking lot outside to show their respect to a man everybody liked and many loved. In the middle of the Pacific on a cloudless star-filled night, thousands of miles from anywhere, his younger son grieved his loss.

In the days that followed, I saw that for Chris, I'd largely gone missing since my father's death. He had judged the situation with a maturity beyond his years, giving me the space I needed to cope. But I'd almost disappeared from the boat. I was turning up to row but contributing nothing else to the voyage. If there's one thing almost as bad as being bereaved on an ocean rowing boat, it's being the rowing partner of that person.

I knew it was my job to get Chris to San Francisco. He deserved better than a grieving wreck as a rowing partner. He was putting his life on the line to achieve our ambition. I owed him my best efforts. I needed to contribute more to the boat and to the success of the project. I needed to snap out of my grief. I began to think I might know a way to do just that.

Chris had stowed a ten-pound bag of rice in the boat before we left. I wouldn't have taken it, instead packing more ready-to-eat rations. For every aspect of an ocean rowing boat, I looked to keep things simple. Cooking meals from scratch was not simple.

Chris had great respect for the early ocean rowers, who'd taken their own less specialized expedition foods, and was keen to emulate aspects of their voyages. It was good that he did. The locals in Choshi had also made a point of giving us cans of corned beef as gifts for our trip under the impression that the average Englishmen ate it every day. That turned out to be a very lucky misconception for us.

As August dawned, it was obvious that we were making slower progress than we'd hoped. To make matters worse, salt water had corrupted some of the supplies stored in the deck lockers. We needed to conserve rations in case the trip took longer than we'd planned, so it made sense to extend them.

I had a great idea: while we were stuck on the parachute anchor, I'd cook something using the corned beef and rice. It would be a break from the routine, replace a couple of regular meals, and hopefully go some way to improving morale on board. It might also help me emerge from my grief.

The next day I set about creating a culinary masterpiece. It took a couple of hours to complete as it wasn't boil-in-the-bag cooking. I had to use pots and pans, and the process was time-consuming and a bit of a juggling act—in itself a welcome distraction. When it was finished, I presented Chris with my corned beef and rice creation. I cleverly called it "corned beef and rice." It was as basic as it was delicious, the first meal we'd eaten on a plate in three months. Up to that point everything had been boiled in and eaten out of a bag. Because of the ample supply of rice, it was a much bigger portion than we were used to. It felt like a feast to our shrinking stomachs. There were even seconds.

Chris was delighted with my cooking efforts and instantly vowed to create another, even finer dish the following day. I wasn't sure how he was going to manage that, given that the available ingredients were corned beef and rice. But he was confident and the next day got to work.

The process had already achieved its principal goal: morale on board had soared for both of us just with the break from normal routine. Any gustatory enjoyment would be a bonus.

Chris finally announced his masterpiece.

"What is it?" I asked.

"Corned beef balls!" he replied proudly.

Usually, when somebody on an ocean rowing boat starts talking about "corned beef balls," they're referring to a painful medical condition that develops with the constant chafing, combined with rowing naked hour after hour. Frankly, Chris's dish didn't look that dissimilar from the medical condition.

It tasted great, though. He'd found some Tabasco sauce, which gave the dish a kick. The atmosphere on the boat was transformed. For the first time since the dreadful loss of my dad, I felt capable of carrying on.

God bless Chris's corned beef balls!

THE MIDNIGHT SHUFFLE

AFTER I'd managed to find a way to battle through the grief of losing my dad, there still remained the battle to reach San Francisco.

August would prove to be a frustrating month despite the better mood on board. It would be successful in terms of progress but not as much as we'd hoped. It was the peak of summer and the month, along with September, when we'd hoped to make the most distance toward our goal. They would be the months we made the most mileage, but not to the extent we'd counted on.

August also brought two unexpected and unwelcome gales. As luck would have it, they would both blow from the southwest, so we could make some progress in front of them. By that time our rowing skills, particularly in heavy weather, had become so good that we managed to row the boat in winds sometimes gusting up to 45 knots. It helped that we had moonlit nights when the gales hit in August and they came with steady rain, which with its impact and weight took some of the edge off the huge seas, but it was still like holding a tiger by the tail.

We trailed a variety of improvised drogues from the stern of our boat. They varied in size from the old woolen seat covers, which were worn out and no longer effective in preventing chafe tied together on the end of a long line, to the para anchor fully inverted and strapped together like a closed hammock. That wasn't how it was designed to be used, but it worked. As the storm gathered strength, we needed a bigger drogue, it fitted the bill. Keeping the stern of the boat facing into the oncoming waves would help us avoid a potentially catastrophic capsizing.

We developed a system at the nighttime changeovers during those terrific storms that we called the "midnight shuffle." It was impossible to hear each other speak over the roar of the wind and waves, so one guy would come out of the cabin and position himself in front of the hatch opposite the rowing seat. You could easily tell which of us was about to finish rowing because he would be smiling manically. The one coming out of the cabin with two hours of rowing in Armageddon to look forward to would not be.

Two safety support lines ran waist high from the cabin roof aft either side to the outer edge of the cabin roof forward. Whoever was taking over would stoop low and hold the lines so as not to be caught out by the waves, which would slam into and frequently over the boat in the darkness. The rower would then pull the oars in, hastily secure them in front of him, and stand, albeit stooped heavily against the elements. We would face each other like two undernourished sumo wrestlers.

On a nod, we'd shuffle around like synchronized swimmers, head to head in a tight circle at the center of the boat, until each of us was in the other's original position. Whoever had just finished rowing would invariably then escape rapidly into the safety of the cabin like a scalded cat, leaving the guy taking over staring incredulously at the vast roaring sea towering above the stern of the boat.

Possibly the most surprising thing about that regularly repeated scenario was that within a couple of minutes in the rowing position, it became normal, even exhilarating, and they were certainly the fastest two-hour shifts we ever experienced. We were now very good ocean rowers. We needed to be; summer was coming to an end, and winter was looming.

After the unexpected storms of August, September thankfully began on a much brighter note. We were looking at almost eight hundred miles made good as we approached the beginning of the third week. That was by far our best progress since leaving the Kuroshio behind. We were rapidly closing in on a thousand miles from the coast of the United States, which, in the context of the vast Pacific Ocean, to us seemed to signal the home stretch.

We'd now rowed farther than I'd managed in my unsuccessful solo crossing in 2004, well over five thousand miles. We were past the point where Tim and Dom, the two serving Royal Marines, had come to grief when run down by an errant fishing boat in 2001. "The downhill stretch," Dom had once said to me. "We were sunk just as we reached the downhill stretch."

Chris and I were about to discover that on the North Pacific there is no downhill stretch. The ocean has you at its mercy until the moment you get off it. What lay ahead of us as we raced through the first two weeks of September, full of optimism, was the hardest two months of both of our lives. The physical and mental challenges of the next two months at sea would dwarf those of the four and a half months that had preceded them.

After we'd eaten all the corned beef and rice, we'd been reducing our food intake to ensure that we'd have enough left to get into San Francisco if it took longer than the six months we'd anticipated. We'd gone from a diet of well over 5,000 calories a day, consisting of four main meals a day and a night snack pack, to three smaller meals with one snack pack per day by mid-September. That was a drop in calories of around a third. As a consequence, we were losing weight.

The corned beef and rice specials we'd consumed to such good effect during our time on the sea anchor, along with some other canned treats, had prolonged the rations by an extra few days. Now the strict rationing was extending our supply. But besides our weight loss, we were fighting a constant battle with salt water.

It didn't matter if the food was double-sealed in an inside locker. Every so often we'd open a bag to find it totally rotten because of a small amount of salt water that had gotten in. We'd been at sea for over four months now. Everything was getting worn out: the boat, the equipment, us. The ration packs were no exception. They were not fully waterproof even inside double-sealed packs. I estimate we'd lost more than three weeks' supply to that problem. By the middle of September, the food loss was becoming a serious issue.

We constantly repacked and rearranged the boat as we ate into our food supply. We kept the stores as we always did, low and central in the boat with more toward the aft (rear) part of the boat. Thick black trash bags filled with seawater placed in the central lockers made up for the weight we'd lost in the lockers as we'd eaten through our supply of largely boil-in-the-bag rations. In heavy weather, we would add to that with more seawater ballast.

We threw no litter overboard. Every used boil-in-the-bag package was restowed in the lockers on deck, which were steadily being depleted of our dwindling daily rations. The only exception to the no-litter rule were the few cans we'd taken. I insisted that they go over the side. With the constant packing and repacking of the lockers, it would be only a matter of time before one of us in our exhausted state sliced his hand on an old can.

I didn't want to throw any rubbish into the ocean, and Chris was even more insistent that we not do so. But a forgotten rusty old can buried deep in a locker full of trash could have created a medical emergency for us. I wasn't prepared to jeopardize all the work we'd done by taking that risk. It eased my conscience a little to see how quickly the cans' cheap metal deteriorated when exposed to seawater, but only a little.

Despite the increasing reduction in calories in our daily diet and the constant battle with corrupted rations, as we sped through those early weeks of September we really began to believe we'd reach the Golden Gate Bridge on schedule and well before the end of October. That would be comfortably before lack of rations or winter weather would become an issue. If the progress we'd made in early September had continued, that could have been the case.

But it didn't. After our best two weeks in months, the North Pacific stopped us in our tracks for the next two weeks.

The wind backed around to blow from the east, where it stayed almost solidly for the remainder of September, halting our progress. It eased off for short periods, usually just long enough for us to retrieve the para anchor and recover a few of the miles we'd lost being pushed backward. Then it would kick in again and steal back those same miles.

It felt as if the monster we'd come to know as the North Pacific was playing games with us. Think of an adult holding a fist-swinging toddler at bay with a hand on his forehead. However hard we swung, we never seemed any closer to landing a blow. When we finally made some progress, it seemed we'd only been allowed to do so to demonstrate how easily we could then be pushed back.

With the nights becoming steadily longer, the North Pacific was taking on an even more menacing air. Our equipment was wearing out, the boat was wearing out, and the temperature of the water and the piercing winds that dogged our progress was starting to drop. Winter was coming.

We'd lost our most important race. We weren't going to beat the North Pacific winter into San Francisco. It was a terrifying thought as we sat on the deck of our boat more than a thousand miles from our destination, slowly being pushed backward.

HOW MUCH MORE
CAN WE TAKE?

FOR LARGE PARTS OF THE SUMMER we'd had to endure stifling heat, in its own way as crippling to a rower as the cold. Shade had been our most precious commodity then. As we slipped into October, shade was no longer an issue. Warmth was our new priority. Whereas during the summer months we'd largely rowed either naked or with simply a surfing top on to fend off the sun's damaging rays, we were now searching the boat for any extra layers of clothing to protect us against the increasing cold. On each shift we were now wearing about eight layers of clothing, every item we possessed. We supplemented them with orange survival suits from our emergency kit, to keep the wind and rain at bay. Our clothing was completely worn out and as porous to the rain that regularly hammered down on us as it was to the increasingly biting winds.

Up until the end of September, I'd never used my sleeping bag. I'd simply slept underneath my foul-weather jacket (which I called Big Red) with my fleece rolled up as a pillow. Chris had used his sleeping bag from the start, along with a full-sized pillow he'd brought along. That pillow had become my nemesis as the voyage progressed. It was bulky and constantly in the way in the cabin, and worst of all, Chris had developed an alarming habit of drooling quite heavily in his sleep. Over the months my nemesis became saturated with that unpleasant leakage. I lost count of how many times I woke from sleep, horrified to find my face fully embedded in that soggy wet mass. Chris swore by that pillow. I swore at it.

By the end of September my foul-weather jacket was a shadow of its former self and more often than not soaking wet. With the temperatures dropping, I dug into the cabin lockers to retrieve my sleeping bag. We'd named Chris's sleeping bag May, after the month he'd started using it. By the end of the fourth month at sea, May had seen better days. By September, she was effectively a stinking skin of a sleeping bag.

As my brand-spanking-new, fresh-smelling fluffy bag of warmth emerged from the locker, her wonderfully clean odor filling the cabin, she was naturally christened September, after the month of her birth. Chris's face was a picture. He reached out to touch the material of what was then the only pristine item remaining on the boat. I batted his hand away. "You can bloody well get your hands off September," I snapped in mock anger. "And keep that scabby pillow of yours away from her, too! September's all mine."

It was a relief to be able to joke about our conditions inside the comparatively safe confines of the cabin. Outside, the reality of our situation darkened as the increasingly shortening days heralded the onset of winter and the ferocious weather it would bring.

We continued the two-hours-on, two-hours-off rowing routine despite the increasingly bitter conditions. It had never been more important to make every available mile east despite the undoubted toll it was taking on us both. The only break to that daily routine was "splitting the dogs," a naval term for two one-hour watches between

6 p.m. and 8 p.m. That meant our shift times reversed every day, so we never rowed the same watch two days running. It also meant that one day we rowed thirteen hours and the next we rowed eleven. We came to regard the eleven-hour day as a day off.

We shared all of our meals. That was built into the watch system. At set times of the day, the guy coming off watch would immediately cook the meal and then the two of us would eat together. It didn't take long, and it was an important way of remaining social. With the relentless rowing routine we were employing and our constant exhaustion, it would have been very easy to lead solo existences on board. Losing a few minutes at the oars each day while we ate together was far outweighed by the benefits.

At the start of the dog watches one day early in October, I retreated to the cabin, freezing cold, soaking wet, and totally exhausted. An hour later, I'd have to go back out again for the second hour of the dog watch, during which Chris would cook the food on deck and we'd eat together. After that I'd have another two hours off. It was my turn for the "day off."

As I sat in the relatively warm cabin, drying off, I looked out at Chris, who was battling the increasingly rain-sodden conditions outside. It was freezing cold, and he was soaking wet under dark gray clouds, which were regularly treating him to fresh downpours. The only positive of the day was that the wind was almost behind us, gently nudging us in the right direction.

As my hour of comfort came to an end, I moved to get out of the cabin. A sudden crescendo on the roof signaled the latest torrential downpour.

Chris shouted, "Stay in there, mate! Don't bother coming out in this for an hour. It's pointless."

I opened the hatch. "I can't do that, mate, it's my watch."

"Look, mate, it's pissing down," he replied. "I'm soaking already, the boat's being blown in the right direction anyway, so we won't lose much distance. There's no point you coming out here to get soaking wet again for forty-five minutes' rowing."

It was as generous a gesture as it was typical of Chris's nature. I was reluctant to accept the offer, though, as it broke our iron code of rowing whenever possible and standing our watch. I knew it made sense, though. I just wished it could have been me outside offering Chris the favor.

That in itself defines the strength of our partnership on board and why we were such an effective and ultimately unbreakable team. Each of us put the other's welfare first. When you look after your partner, the group is stronger. It was a characteristic I'd seldom come across since leaving the Royal Marines. The fact that Chris possessed that characteristic as a natural part of his makeup spoke volumes for him. The marines had had to teach me to behave like that. Chris did it as a matter of course.

To my everlasting regret, at a later critical stage of the voyage I would fail to spot a problem with Chris's welfare, and my negligence would nearly kill him.

WHALE TALES

AS WE ENTERED what would be the last stages of our Pacific row, I began to notice a big difference from my previous solo expedition: apart from a single fleeting glance of a white-and-black dorsal fin hundreds of yards away early in the voyage, we'd seen no killer whales.

Killer whales had been the highlight of my solo Pacific voyage in 2004. I had effectively been adopted by a pod of orcas that had visited me regularly throughout the voyage. The first time I had come into contact with them, I didn't even realize they were killer whales. It was the evening of June 13, the day after my fortieth birthday. The sun had only just set, combining with the clouds to create a dramatic purple-and-orange backdrop to the rapidly encroaching darkness. Suddenly two huge dorsal fins emerged completely unheralded from beneath the surface of the ocean, only inches from the back of my boat, one, bizarrely, leaning over lopsidedly, both fins taller than the roof of the cabin, which they were next to. My first thought was "Sharks!" But two rapid and powerful blasts of air dispelled that misconception. "Whales!" I still had no idea what species they were, though, and tried to identify them while I grabbed my camera to film our strange twilight encounter. In the meantime, they drifted slowly into the darkness.

A few days later, while rowing at daybreak, I looked over my shoulder to see, no more than fifty yards away, large black dorsal fins, maybe a dozen of them, emerging like a fleet of periscopes from the surface of the ocean. As soon as I saw the first flash of white, I realized the identity of my earlier visitors: they were killer whales. The pod was heading in the opposite direction from me. As they passed, two of the animals broke away and swam straight toward me. Obviously youngsters but both still as big as my boat, they hurtled toward me just beneath the crystal clear waters. One peeled off at the last moment and sped around the front of my boat. The other swam to within inches from the hull of my boat, directly beneath where I now stood filming. I spun around to capture his departure on the other side, but the animal stopped right next to my boat, effortlessly pirouetted, then surfaced, staring straight at me. It was the most incredible experience; I could have reached out and touched that spectacular creature, it was so close. Finally, with a blast of air, it sank down beneath the surface once more, spun on its tail, and took off after its departing pod, leaping out of the water as it did so. It was a remarkable encounter, one of many I would have with the same pod of whales during my solo voyage in 2004, all caught on the film I lost during my subsequent capsize and rescue.

One encounter that wasn't captured on film but remains indelibly etched on my memory occurred a few hours after that first meeting with the orcas. The glorious purple-and-orange sunset had been replaced by a veil of near-impenetrable darkness. The clouds that, in tandem with the sun, had helped create such a vivid backdrop to my whale visit were now conspiring to withhold the reassuring light of the stars and the moon. Following my course, now visible only as a lighted heading on the compass fitted above the cabin door, my boat and I continued to draw our way, one heavy stroke at a time, across the greatest ocean in the world. the only break in the darkness a weak circle of light created by the single white navigation light just above my head, directly behind me on the bow of the boat.

Understandably on a high after the excitement brought about by my earlier unexpected guests and eager to build on what was a good day's progress, I decided to continue rowing well into the night before cooking and eating my evening meal. Then I'd row again into the early hours before grabbing a short sleep just ahead of daybreak. Three hours into my plans and with the ocean still a flat calm, I noticed some frantic activity beneath the hull of my boat.

That was by no means an unusual or initially an alarming event, as darkness was always dinnertime for somebody in the ocean. Curious, I pulled in both my oars and prepared to witness what I presumed was someone else's supper.

It's worth explaining at this stage that since it had been a long, hot, exhausting days' work, I'd reduced my clothing to the bare minimum to avoid chafe and overheating. In fact, most of the day I'd been rowing naked, and even several hours into the night, I'd resorted to only a single short-sleeved surfing top to maintain my dignity and body heat. As I'm sure you can imagine, this partial state of undress only served to intensify my feelings of vulnerability when I saw, directly alongside my boat, a shape not unlike a very large snake swim by.

The creature was at least two meters long and as thick at its middle as an anaconda. I couldn't believe my eyes and at first put it down to a trick of the poor light—until I saw, only moments later, another of the creatures swim by, then another followed by another, all just below the surface of the water, menacingly within touching distance. It appeared that my dimly lit rowing boat had somehow become the focal point of a large group of predators that had seemingly leapt from the pages of an ancient mariners' drunken tale.

By this stage of the voyage, I had attracted a motley crew of glum-looking fish beneath the hull of *Mrs D* that I had come to describe as my "tenants." They'd apparently—although, as it turned out, mistakenly—seen the shadow of the hull as a safe haven from the many and varied predators of the North Pacific; in fairness to them, up to that point they'd been proved right. However, the arrival of those terrifying creatures must have come as an even greater shock to them than it did to me, because for the next five or ten minutes I watched, secure on the deck of my rowing boat and within arm's length of them, as they decimated my tenants and presumably any other unfortunate sea creatures they stumbled upon.

It was a sight as terrifying as it was hypnotic; they were without doubt the most aggressive predators I'd ever seen at sea—or on land, for that matter. Moving like gray lightning bolts through the water, they hit their hapless prey and seemed to engulf then like boa constrictors, their whole bodies folding into what seemed like seething knots on impact. It was as awe-inspiring as the emergence of the two whales earlier in the evening but with a far greater sense of menace. For the first time in the trip I didn't think to reach for the camera; for the first time I was genuinely unnerved, and filming what was happening was the last thing on my mind.

On the deck of the boat in the darkness, I still couldn't convince myself of what I was seeing. The creatures appeared to be large conger eels, probably as many as seven or eight of them, but I was a thousand miles off the coast of Japan, with several miles of ocean beneath me. Surely conger eels didn't roam the ocean in predatory groups like that. As the last of my unlucky "tenants" received their eviction orders, the activity in the water around my boat decreased before finally coming to an end.

I am not embarrassed to admit that the encounter had left me a little anxious. The episode had come as a complete surprise; it was certainly unlike any of my previous wildlife encounters, and then as now I couldn't fully explain what I'd seen. I sat back on the rowing seat looking out into the darkness, hoping to locate the unusual assassins once more so I could identify them, when, to my horror, little more than an oar's length away, I saw one of the creatures, head raised eighteen inches out of the water, staring directly back at me. I couldn't believe my eyes, and to compound my mounting terror, when I looked to my left, two more of them were elevated above the surface of the ocean, their gaze intently fixed on me, one no more than a couple of meters away.

In the inky darkness all I could see was the red eyes of the creatures, together with what seemed like the tips of their noses, reflected in the dim glow of my navigation light. Their heads, about the size of a small dog, appeared, as far as I could make out, reptilian. For a few seconds I even tried to convince myself that I was looking at sea turtles, albeit very large ones. The gray outline of their coiled bodies just beneath the surface of the water and their sudden rapid movements dispelled that thought, however; they were not turtles, they were the creatures that had so ably disposed of my tenants.

Then, just as I thought the growing nightmare couldn't get any worse—one of them hissed.

"You are fucking joking!" I said to no one in particular.

It rapidly became apparent to me that sitting within striking distance of those highly aggressive predators, which had suddenly developed a curiosity about me, was not the wisest course of action, especially practically naked. So slowly and under the constant gaze of my visitors, I stood up in the near darkness and stepped over my oars—which were strapped, unhelpfully, across the deck of my boat. I proceeded to make my way cautiously from the rowing position toward the sanctuary of the cabin entrance toward the rear of the boat. My "nest" had never been more appealing. I don't think I'd ever been more acutely aware of the possible consequences of falling over-board into the sea as I gingerly, one deliberate step at a time, made my way along the rolling deck of my rowing boat.

In response, my visitors repeatedly hissed and continued to shift position, like amphibious meerkats, disappearing beneath the surface and then, a second later, reappearing nearby in that same erect menacing stance. I never saw more than three of them with their heads above the water at the same time, but I did see the gray flashes of other bodies swimming rapidly beneath the boat on either side, so I knew there were still a substantial number surrounding me.

The short distance between the rowing position and the cabin, which I normally would have covered in a couple of bounds, had now developed into a much more challenging and altogether more worrying proposition. Anxious not to overexcite my guests or quite literally rock the boat, I was moving as slowly and deliberately as possible. However, ocean rowing boats rock even in the lightest of conditions. To my now-heightened senses my vessel had the stability of a lumberjack's tumbling log.

Eventually, however, and mightily relieved, I finally managed to step down into the foot well in front of the cabin hatch unmolested. I promptly pulled on a pair of "protective" running shorts, which, although unquestionably inadequate for the job at hand, substantially reduced my feelings of vulnerability. With my confidence and to some extent dignity restored and with the sanctuary of the lockable cabin directly behind me, I retrieved a flashlight and a diving knife with which to confront my tormentors. The laughably small diving knife was more Swiss Army than Croc' Dundee, equally as inadequate as the running shorts, but strangely, just as reassuring. I opened the hatch, stepped back into it with one foot, in case a rapid retreat was required, and shone the flashlight out into the dark.

My visitors continued to surround me, regularly appearing above the surface in ones, twos, and occasionally threes, if anything growing bolder all the time, and emphasizing their presence with those disturbing hisses or sudden bursts of activity on the surface of the water.

After several minutes of the increasingly unnerving activity, I was mightily relieved to discover that shining the flashlight directly at the creatures seemed to discourage their advances. Every time the beam landed on one of them, it would immediately reposition itself just outside it, as if scolded by its glare. By repeating that with the flashlight, I eventually managed to create a small, circular, "serpent-free" zone around the boat, at least on the surface.

It was a relief to see their reaction to the light, and for the first time since they'd emerged above the surface of the water, obviously to investigate me, I felt that I might be able to discourage them from getting into the boat if they chose to do so.

After what must have been thirty or forty minutes of this bizarre maritime Mexican standoff, my tormentors, who were becoming increasingly reluctant to be caught in the flashlight beam, finally and thankfully departed. Perhaps they tired of me, or maybe they simply went in search of less troublesome and more recognizable prey; either way and much to my relief, they disappeared as suddenly as they'd arrived.

Despite the undignified position of one leg in, one leg out of the cabin and every sinew of my body telling me to lock myself in the cabin, I'd managed to remain on the deck throughout the strange encounter. It had genuinely disturbed me, though, so I decided to reassess my plans to row into the night. I could make the mileage up tomorrow. In the daylight. Instead I settled for cooking and eating a meal from the protective confines of my cabin, fully clothed. Nakedness had lost its novelty, and the deck area, where I usually sat while cooking, had even less appeal. Uncharacteristically but probably not unsurprisingly, I also decided on an early night, "safe" in the secure confines of my cabin from anything else the sleepy Pacific Ocean had to offer, at least for the time being.

What were my visitors? I still honestly don't know. Possibly seals or sea lions? That was a plausible explanation, especially when combined with the pitch black conditions and my level of exhaustion. At the time, though, much like my first theory about their being turtles, I remember ruling that possibility out, so I'm not convinced. A marine biologist whom I consulted when I returned couldn't provide a definitive answer, either, although he did say, "The Pacific is a massive ocean, and nobody goes where you were on such a small vessel, so close to the surface, moving so slowly. Especially at night. There's a lot out there we haven't seen; maybe you've seen something we've not documented yet."

Who knows? One thing's for sure: if those serpents, or whatever they were, had returned that night, they'd have had to work out how to unlock my cabin door and unzip my sleeping bag before I went back on the menu.

In 2009, I'm relieved to say, there was no reappearance of the "sea serpents," and, much more disappointingly, our encounters with whales were also far less numerous and certainly not at such close quarters as on my previous voyages.

The one notable exception to that was in September, when a huge sperm whale powered toward the boat just after dawn. Steaming along the surface of the ocean, it was clearly intent on investigating the strange new addition to its world. After a powerful and increasingly intimidating approach, the animal stopped inches from the back of the boat. It checked us out in detail, its huge, bulbous head emerging out of the water. Obviously unimpressed, it sank below the surface, turned slightly on its axis, and headed off into the distance. It was a fabulous encounter with the biggest predator the world has ever seen, but it was relatively brief and nothing as intense as my experiences with the killer whales in 2004. It wouldn't be the last encounter we'd have with whales during the voyage.

We'd been making steady progress since emerging from September's stalling conditions. The rowing was hard, and the weather was noticeably colder. Everything was an effort. The end of the row could not come quickly enough. It's some indication of our state of mind that one morning when I came out to relieve Chris at six o'clock, the last part of his handover to me was "Oh, by the way, we've got a whale hanging around with us."

Right on cue, a whale twenty yards off our starboard side fired a burst of water and air out of its blowhole. I was immediately covered in a cloud of whale snot, which stank of fish. That was a great start to the watch. Neither of us batted an eye.

As Chris enjoyed the start of his well-earned rest in the cabin, I settled in for another two hours at the oars. Our stalker, apart from the fishy welcome, had not been very active once I'd come on watch, so I didn't give him much thought.

Then I started to notice a little more activity in the water. I looked over and saw an even bigger whale, perhaps twice the size of our boat, racing through the water just below the surface, heading straight toward us at high speed.

"Bloody hell!"

The whale passed beneath the boat, inches from making contact, then began to circle our position. As it did so, another, slightly smaller whale joined it. "Bloody hell, there's two of them."

Then I saw a third whale surface on the other side of the boat. I wasn't sure what species they were, but they all looked the same. They appeared to be a blue-green color under the water with a lighter-colored lower-body section. There were two larger creatures, I assumed the adults, and one smaller, presumably their calf. The biggest of them was over forty feet long, the calf a little longer than our boat. For some reason our vessel had become the focal point of their attention.

They continued to circle at impressive speeds just below the surface of the water, regularly charging toward the boat, either sinking just below the surface as they reached me or peeling off at the last second and heading in front of or behind Bo.

Reluctantly, because not interrupting anyone's sleep unless it was an emergency was a golden rule on the boat, I called out to Chris, "Mate, there are three whales out here. You've got to come and see this."

As bleary-eyed and pissed-off-looking a Chris Martin as it's possible for his agreeable nature to allow eventually emerged from the cabin. "This had better be good," he growled.

It was. The three whales, which we'd later learn were sei whales, stayed with us for the next six and a half hours. They never seemed to tire of either us or their rapid underwater flybys. Occasionally they crashed into each other in what seemed like some sort of game, but as close as they got to us at times—within inches—they never made contact with our boat. The boat, however, did make contact with them.

I was rowing through my second shift after their arrival. The whales, which had been around for nearly six hours by then, had taken to charging the boat, peeling off at the last second, then stopping directly in front of us, almost as if they didn't want us to go. But we had to go, we needed to keep making every possible mile east. As once more a charging whale peeled off in front of the boat, I pulled steadily on the oars.

A second or two later there was a horrible feeling similar to rowing a boat up a beach as the boat ground to a halt on top of the largest of the three whales. Amazingly, Chris felt it and immediately pushed the hatch open and shouted from the cabin, "Enjoy your swim, I'm locking the hatch!" before slamming it shut and securing himself safely inside.

I grimaced and braced, waiting for the inevitable impact as a powerful tail swept me and the boat off the whale's back. It didn't come. The whale sank down in the water and slowly moved off. An hour or so later they finally grew bored with us and disappeared into the endless miles of the Pacific.

They weren't killer whales, but they had been spectacular and had treated us to a memorable experience. It served to remind us both that despite the hardships we were enduring, we were incredibly privileged to be doing what we were doing.

Up to the point when news of my father's passing came through, there was nowhere in the world I'd rather have been than rowing the North Pacific. From that day onward it was the last place I wanted to be, simply a challenge I was stubbornly determined to finish. No longer a joy, it had become a prison sentence.

Those hours sharing that unique experience with the three whales reminded me again why I was there. They had lifted me out of the war we were now fighting to get to San Francisco and shone some sunlight on our trials. I felt rejuvenated. Perhaps the North Pacific wasn't as spiteful as I thought?

At any moment of any day, something as magical and thrilling as that could happen out on that great ocean. How many people in the world could wish for such an opportunity, let alone expect one? I always described our row, no matter how low I felt, as having the best seats at the best show in town.

It did. The only drawback was how hard you had to work to earn the tickets.

34

THE DEATH ZONE

THE END OF SEPTEMBER brought some good news: we finally crossed the thousand-miles-to-go mark, although by that time we were under no illusions that there was any downhill stretch. The day we crossed that imaginary line in the ocean came with mixed blessings.

My wife, Grace, who'd gone to the United Kingdom on a six-month tourist visa, was in my absence refused an extension. That meant that unless our pace improved dramatically, she would have to return to Nigeria before I got home. It was bitterly upsetting for Grace and yet another stab in the heart for me.

Bureaucracy being what it is, particularly in regard to immigration, there was apparently no room for either sentiment or flexibility. As a desperate last effort, my family contacted our local member of Parliament to see if he could negotiate an exception under the circumstances, just until I got back from rowing across the North Pacific, something we felt might allow for an exception of a few days. Grace even went for a meeting with him, in which he was apparently very charming and supportive. (His letter telling us that there was, sadly, nothing he could do arrived several weeks after I returned home.)

As disheartening as that news was, like everything that happened at home, on the boat we had to distance ourselves from it and focus on getting to San Francisco. Our lives had been at stake since we left Japan, but never more so as we stared into the face of the approaching North Pacific winter.

As October stretched before us, we knew we faced at the very least another month at sea. Burning emotional energy worrying about issues at home that we could in no way influence would only worsen our already precarious situation.

The death of my Dad had left me with a fierce determination to smash through anything that now stood in my way. If I could get through that, I reasoned, I could get through anything. I'd get through the bad news about the visa, and I'd get through anything else that was thrown at me. That fierce determination would prove to be both a blessing and a curse in the dramatic weeks ahead.

Meanwhile, our food situation was becoming increasingly serious, particularly as every unfavorable weather report, which at that time appeared to be almost every weather report, extended our arrival date by a day or two. Our already reduced three-meals-a-day rations were now further reduced to two, and the mealtimes for which there was no longer any food were replaced by "a hot wet," our vernacular for a cup of tea, or, on a particularly miserable day, the rare treat of one of our last remaining hot chocolates.

There still seemed the faint possibility of a late-October finish. But that would require luck with the weather for the first time in five months. We started to make plans for how we might take supplies off passing ships if the chance arose. There would likely be more opportunity for that now, as we were approaching land and the main shipping routes again. It seemed a sensible precaution.

Over in the United Kingdom, my Atlantic rowing partner, Mos, and an old work colleague and friend, Amanda Claridge, had slipped into becoming our shore support team. I'd never actually looked much beyond arriving in San Francisco. Now, as desperate as our situation seemed to Chris and me out on the Pacific, to Mos and Amanda it appeared that we might actually make it. They figured we might need some help, and they were right.

I updated Mos regularly on our progress and conditions on board. He knew what life on an ocean rowing boat was like, particularly with me, so he developed a lot of sympathy for Chris. We made preliminary plans for resupply if we couldn't grab stuff off a passing ship or, if the worse came to the worst, an emergency recovery. Those were plans I hoped would always remain theoretical.

Mos, who is the CEO of his own freight company, assured me that one of his clients, a shipping company, had agreed to drop us a resupply the day we decided we needed one. It had ships entering and leaving ports in California regularly, so it wouldn't be a problem. We hoped the weather would finally be kind to us and we wouldn't need those supplies, but we now had the reassurance that we could be resupplied if it were necessary.

For the umpteenth time Chris and I audited the remaining food on board. It was a shorter process than it had been in August because there was less food. We then created a food plan to see us through the remainder of the voyage. It consisted of little more than 1,000 calories a day each, less than a fifth of what we'd been eating when we set out. We'd already lost more than fifty pounds of body weight each, but the weight loss was manageable. Knowing a resupply was at worst forty-eight hours away gave us the confidence to push on.

As we began to close in on land and winter set in, the weather patterns became less helpful. The forecasts lost the reliability they'd had over the long months of summer in the open ocean. We could get a report in the morning that promised us everything we needed for a late-October arrival under the Golden Gate Bridge, only to receive another forecast twelve hours later that suggested we'd be on the sea anchor for the next week. It was an additional mental torture that we could have done without as we dealt with our lengthening list of problems.

As almost every day now seemed to bring a period of time on the para anchor, we were looking for things to break up the monotony after close to six months at sea. We needed to ration our battery power, so music and audiobooks were no longer an option. Our batteries, much like the rest of the equipment on board, were beginning to flag.

"What about this?" Chris said one day.

He held a small metal can in his hand with "Travel Chess/ Draughts" written on the front. "It's a chess set, but I don't really play chess," he said.

The prospect of chess in our current weary mental state held no appeal whatsoever, even if Chris could have played it, but checkers, with its obvious simplicity, did. We were so tired at that point that we were forgetting basic words. I was even forgetting family members' names at times. It was as close to dementia as I ever want to come.

We had a chat one day while stalled on the para anchor about all the things we'd like to do once we had cracked the Pacific. One goal we both had was to travel across the United States in a luxury motor home.

"You know the ones," Chris said, trying to remember the name of the one we envisaged.

I knew exactly the ones he meant. Neither of us could remember the bloody name, though.

We both sat there wracking our brains to remember it but just couldn't access the section of our dehydrated and exhausted brains where that information was stored. That went on for days and became a growing cause of frustration and humor. Sometimes it would be there for a moment, right on the tip of our tongues, but we simply couldn't remember it. That was part of the toll of six months at sea in a rowing boat.

Then one morning, in the middle of my watch, Chris burst out of the cabin grinning and at the top of his voice shouted to the sea, "WINNEBAGO! WINNE-FUCKING-BAGO!"

My feeling of relief at finally hearing the name vocalized was tempered only by an unnatural urge to strangle my friend for remembering it first.

"Let's give the draughts a go, mate," I replied. "We might be able to manage that."

At the height of our war with the North Pacific, Chris and I entered into battle with each other on the checkerboard.

It whiled away hours on the para anchor when we'd have otherwise been worrying about our plight. It improved our morale no end. Well, it improved my morale no end. Ultimately the scoreboard we'd scribbled on the cabin roof would read nine victories for Chris, two of which were highly debatable, in my opinion, fifty-eight victories for me, none debatable. For a time, reaching double figures on that scoreboard had more significance for Chris than rowing under the Golden Gate Bridge.

Apart from the checkers and the extended visit from our three sei whales, there was one other high point in October: an unexpected high-pressure system brought with it unseasonably warm weather as it lingered overhead for a couple of days. We eagerly removed our multiple layers of clothing and reverted to rowing naked again while the sun was up. It allowed us to dry the multiple layers of sodden clothing we'd been living in and air out our saturated cabin. It transformed our existence on board from wretched to difficult, and it couldn't have come at a better time.

Until that point the weather had been getting colder each day. The nights were increasingly long, and we were regularly battered by gales. The storms were stronger, more frequent, and longer than those we'd experienced before. Just living on the boat would have been exhausting. Living on it while rowing around the clock with next to no food after almost half a year at sea was physically, mentally, and emotionally torturous for the pair of us.

The most terrifying thought was that it could get worse. We were out of typhoon range, but now, on the US side of the Pacific in winter, our big worry was being hit by a hurricane.

The unexpected burst of good weather provided a much-needed opportunity for us to recharge not only our own batteries but the boat's batteries as well.

In September, we'd developed what steadily became a major problem with power that had nearly crippled our power system before we discovered exactly what was causing it. We were losing more and more battery power every day until finally the charge fell so low that one morning the system shut down completely.

We had information displayed on the battery management control box in our cabin for everything with the exception of the load on the batteries (the power being drawn by each device connected to them). Time restraints had gotten into the way of that being installed when the boat was being fitted out. By the time I discovered that, it was too late to be put right before she was shipped. It was a foolish omission that would come close to destroying the project.

If we'd had that information readout on the battery management display in the cabin, we'd have immediately picked up on the problem. Early in September, we'd replaced a broken navigation light with a different type of bulb. The draw on the batteries by the new bulb had gone up from barely a fraction of an amp to 1.4 amps, the equivalent of charging a computer all night.

Without the load readout display we couldn't see that. The new navigation light proceeded to slowly suck the life out of our batteries every night we used it. It wasn't just draining all our power but also damaging the batteries' ability to retain a charge.

Chris discovered the cause when he decided to test each device as a last resort. It was a fiddly, time-consuming, awkward job, which was why it was the last resort. But it immediately gave us the answer to our problem: that one lightbulb was chewing up more than half our power every twenty-four hours.

If we'd kept things simple—my own rule, which I hadn't abided by—and done the work before we left despite the time constraints, the issue would never have arisen. Now we were entering the hardest part of the voyage with the added pressure of nursing our dying batteries into San Francisco. I was furious with myself. Looking back, that error was the one thing I'd change in the whole project, the only real mistake I should have avoided.

As fast as the battery power levels were dropping, our energy levels on a starvation diet were dropping much faster. It was a nightmare for both of us to keep up the rowing regime now that hunger, never a stranger to any ocean rower, had become our constant companion.

The winter temperature drop, despite the two-day respite of the high-pressure system, was continuing, and each night's rowing became a mental and physical endurance test. There were no more easy shifts.

Chris, in particular, was beginning to struggle with the cold. He was in his midtwenties, an elite athlete with little body fat to lose, even after bulking up for the trip. What fat he did have was long gone by the end of October, offering him little to draw on for extra energy or insulation.

I, on the other hand, was a middle-aged former Royal Marine. I'd always functioned well in the cold, and putting body fat on in preparation for the row had been much easier for me than for Chris. I still had some reserves to draw on.

The cold might not have been bothering me too much at that point, but I remember that every time I crawled into the cabin after two hours rowing a night watch I doubted my ability to crawl out again in another two hours. Both Chris and I were engaged in the fight of our lives as we struggled through those harsh weeks of October.

There was one ray of hope that promised to ease our misery on the twenty-fifth of the month: we saw a ship's navigation lights looming over the horizon, heading in our direction. I shouted to Chris, "Let's see if we can get them on the VHF and grab some food off them, mate."

Chris leapt to the VHF radio, and within a couple of minutes the ship had answered and agreed to drop off a couple of boxes of supplies. She was called the *Genoa Bridge*, and she was a huge commercial vessel. It couldn't stop unless it was an emergency, and this wasn't one. We told the officers we were hungry and running short of food, but we weren't in a critical situation. We were doing this to offset a potential problem in the future; it was not a Mayday by any means.

They replied that in that case they would have to pass by us and then turn hard right just ahead of us. When we were alongside their center, they would sound their horn and drop a couple of illuminated supply containers into the water. We would maintain the same course and scoop up the containers.

It seemed to me to be a very complicated solution to a really simple problem. However, I understood the pressures on commercial vessels being micromanaged from land. It was part of their ship's protocol, and they weren't able to alter it. Chris and I prepared for the maneuver and the eagerly anticipated arrival of supplies. They'd even promised tea bags.

The ship steamed by in the darkness no more than a hundred yards away from us, the guys on deck cheering as they passed, all the ship's deck lights on. It carried on past us a few hundred yards before swinging hard to the right in the darkness. A few moments later the horn blasted, and our supplies were presumably committed to the sea.

The ship continued back on her original course, and Chris and I scanned the ocean around our boat, trying to locate our booty. On the VHF radio the chief officer, who was from India, checked in to see if we'd picked up the supplies yet.

"Not yet," we replied.

Twenty minutes later, hugely deflated, we finally accepted that the night and the ocean had swallowed up our prize. We expressed our thanks to the unseen chief officer for his and his crew's efforts and slipped dejectedly back into our relentless rowing routine.

Three days later, approaching the last week of our rations, we received a weather forecast from Lee that gave us a straight run into San Francisco. It was fantastic news; if the forecast held, it would see us under the Golden Gate bridge by the fourth or fifth of November at the latest. We wouldn't need a resupply now. It would be close, but we could make it in on the supplies we had left.

I went over the side for the last time to clean the barnacles off the bottom of the boat. That would allow us the best boat speed for the final push to San Francisco. The water was freezing now. Whereas earlier in the voyage it had been a welcome break from the rowing for us both to drop over the side to do the cleaning, having both of us in the water at the same time now was dangerous. It was so cold that it might require someone on deck to pull the other one in. Chris was cold enough rowing that I couldn't expect him to jump into what were now almost arctic waters.

I proceeded to complete the fastest hull clean of the whole trip. I doubt I was in the water for more than six or seven minutes, as opposed to the normal thirty or forty. The last time I'd been in water that cold was during through-the-ice drills in Norway during my arctic training with the marines. Now, when I finished, Chris dragged me back on deck and threw my jacket over me.

"Cold enough for you, mate?" he asked, grinning.

"That's the last time I'm doing that, mate," I gasped.

We grinned manically at each other. We'd finally reached the point in the voyage where we were doing things for the last time.

We were nearly there. Or so we thought.

35

DEVASTATED!

WITH THE PROMISE of helpful winds we drew on what remained of our reserves and set to rowing once more with renewed vigor. Little more than two hundred miles now separated us from the finish line we'd been working so hard to reach. It might still have been out of sight, but we were beginning to convince ourselves that it was within our grasp.

We should have known better. On October 31, we received a devastating new weather forecast.

There was another storm coming in from the north, this one a force 8. It was expected to dominate for at least five days. Slowly veering around to the northeast, it would once again force us to use the para anchor. Our hopes of arriving at the beginning of November disappeared as quickly as our newly upbeat mood.

Worse still, because the storm was going to blow solidly from the north, we now had to race as far east as we could before it stopped us, in order to maintain any hope of eventually making a course into San Francisco. We were going to be blown south for five days! If we were blown too far south, the project was finished; there'd be no way to get to San Francisco. A single weather report had transformed our prospects from imminent success to almost certain failure. We were both utterly devastated.

But being devastated, although understandable, wasn't going to alter our position. The situation had changed. It did that a lot on the North Pacific. We didn't have to like it, but we did need to do something about it.

The first thing we decided was that we'd order the resupply of food from Mos. With at least a five-day delay to any arrival date in San Francisco, there was no question now that we were going to run out of food. At least we'd have fresh supplies to look forward to.

The second thing we needed to do to have any hope of saving the whole project was to push as far east as we could before the storm came in and stopped us. Big winds and seas were coming, so we ballasted the boat down with extra seawater in the black trash bags. We needed to sit as low in the water as we could since we were going to have to row across a northerly gale and the waves it would create to make ground toward the California coast. A drogue wouldn't be as effective in saving us from capsizing now as it had been when we ran directly in front of the waves. Sitting heavy and low in the water would at least give us more stability and some resistance to capsizing.

We also needed to set up both rowing positions. Two of us rowing would give us a little more speed, but more crucially, it would allow us to row against the conditions for longer. It was now all about how many miles east we could row before the storm stopped us. The success of the whole project hung on that mileage. Too few miles, and we'd never make it to San Francisco, because the storm would push us too far south. All our efforts over six months at sea now depended on what we could do in the next twenty-four hours.

It was just before midday on October 31 when we received the bad news—Halloween, appropriately enough. By midday we'd prepared the boat and requested the resupply from Mos. Exactly 206 nautical miles from San Francisco in building seas, Chris and I began pulling on the oars together, starting a desperate race against time.

Nine hours later, utterly exhausted and with the gale raging and freezing winds cutting through us, we decided to break down into a solo rowing routine again so we could at least get some sleep during the night. We'd already passed the position that Lee had suggested would ensure our holding a course into San Francisco. Anything after that was a bonus. We carried on through the night with our relentless two-hours-on, two-hours-off routine until the storm finally swung around to the northeast and stopped us dead in our tracks.

Exhausted, we deployed the parachute anchor and collapsed into the cabin. Bitterly cold in freezing winds, soaking wet, and being broadsided by waves from a growing northerly gale, Chris and I had managed to row more than thirty-three miles east in just under twenty-two grueling hours. It was an enormous effort that had probably saved the whole project, or at the very least kept it alive. But it had taken its toll. We were both shattered.

The following day, as we rode out the storm in the cabin recovering, Chris said to me, "I was so cold last night. I can't do that again, mate."

I'd said exactly the same thing after the last freezing hull clean. We were saying that to each other about pretty much everything we had to do by then. So I laughed, not thinking he was serious.

"Yeah, me neither, mate," I replied and thought no more about it.

I didn't realize how serious he was.

36

WE'RE GOING TO MAKE IT!

TWO DAYS LATER, as we continued to ride out the storm, check-ing on the chart the miles we were losing south on the para anchor, we received a change in the weather forecast. For once it appeared to be in our favor. The storm was going to pass more quickly than anticipated, and there'd be a chance to make ground earlier than we'd expected. We prepped the boat for rowing and checked on the food resupply we'd spoken to Mos about. It had been due that day, weather permitting. With the storm now due to die off, that was now a possibility.

It was indeed a possibility for us but apparently no longer a pos-sibility for the shipping company.

"They've said no, mate," Mos told us dejectedly on the satellite phone. "Somebody has put the kibosh on it at head office, and they won't do it now."

"Mate, we've pushed it this far because they'd promised us a resupply the moment we needed it," I said. "If they weren't able to do it, why didn't they say that from the start?"

"I know, mate, I'm sorry. Leave it with me," he said. "I'll sort something, but there's no chance of a resupply today or tomorrow. I'm sorry."

Mos had nothing to be sorry for. He was doing everything he could to help us. The person at the shipping company who'd made the promise should have been apologizing.

We had sixteen meals and snack packs left, with no way of knowing when we'd next get food. We reviewed our food schedule and adjusted it once more to try to sustain our efforts while we waited for a resupply date. We settled on half a meal each at 8 a.m. and 4 p.m. and a hot wet and emergency biscuits at noon and midnight. The biscuits, which we'd liberated from the emergency pack, were highly caloric but tasteless. Still, in our present situation they were a welcome addition to our dwindling stock of food. That would allow us eight more days with at least some semblance of rations to rely on.

As our food supply diminished, we attempted to supplement our diet with fish. Suffice it to say, our attempts were not a success. Whenever we tried to fish, there was not a fish in sight or the fish we did attract were completely indifferent to our efforts. At one stage we watched dorado swim up to the silver lures we were using for bait on our hooks and actually spit them out before we could hook them. And those were normally fish famed for practically throwing themselves on your line. We would have been better served with a harpoon, no offense to our sei whale friends.

With our conspicuous lack of success below the waterline, Chris began to raise his sights higher. "What about killing an albatross?" he asked sinisterly one day, watching one of our constant companions fly by.

I looked quizzically at him. "You're not very familiar with maritime superstitions, are you mate?"

He looked back at me and frowned. He apparently wasn't very familiar with poetry, either. Samuel Taylor Coleridge's lengthy nineteenth-century poem "The Rime of the Ancient Mariner" is about the dire consequences to sailors of killing an albatross.

"I think we might keep that as a final option," I said.

As disappointing as the news on the food front was, the brightening of the weather forecast was a major plus. With less than two hundred miles to our destination, we were as close as anyone had ever come to pulling off this world "first." It was going to be tough, but San Francisco was within our grasp again. We just had to find a way to keep going.

After hauling the boat east through a roaring gale a couple of days earlier, the break in weather seemed like just deserts for our labors. Our mood lifted yet again, and once more we both found the energy to get back on the oars. We were starting to believe that we'd earned our run to the Golden Gate Bridge.

The North Pacific thought differently. As we struck off on an easterly heading, it placed ahead of us what would be our greatest challenge yet

We dragged the para anchor in by 11 a.m. on October 2, and by 5:30 p.m. the same day we found ourselves once more headed into the wind, not a gale but blowing close to 15 knots, strong enough to stop us. We wearily deployed the parachute anchor for what we hoped would be the last time and prepared to wait out the wind.

As soon as the anchor was in place, we realized that we were in a current dragging us steadily southwest, exactly the wrong direction. We immediately heaved the anchor back in and did our best to row any heading east that didn't send us backward and, we hoped, would eventually lead us out of the current. In our present physical condition, it was backbreaking work just to set and retrieve the anchor.

Having to do it and then row against the newly discovered current and the wind was deeply demoralizing.

We couldn't believe that exhausted, soaking wet, and freezing cold, we would be unable to ride out the adverse winds on the anchor. If we didn't keep rowing, we'd be forced southwest by the current and the wind, eventually reaching a point where it would be impossible to make it into San Francisco. For what seemed the thousandth time, we looked into ourselves for another reserve of strength and willpower and took to the oars.

We rowed through the rest of the day and into the bitterly cold night, battling desperately to extricate ourselves from the current, a band of freezing Alaskan water flowing snakelike south down the coast of California. It was an Arctic version of the Kuroshio we'd left behind all those months ago. It was no more than thirty miles across at its widest point, and we needed to get out of it as quickly as possible. If we didn't, it would drag us relentlessly south and ultimately to failure.

After another herculean effort during eighteen hours of constant rowing, we found ourselves approaching what had to be the edge of the current. We were nearly there. A mile or two further, and we'd be out of the current and off that conveyor belt south.

Once more, at the point of salvation, the North Pacific at her meanest and most spiteful conjured up another easterly wind and stopped us dead in our tracks. It wasn't even a particularly strong wind, just enough that it made it impossible for us to row east.

I prayed that the distance being lost shown on the GPS was because of the wind, not the current. I secured my oars. At the limit of my energy reserves, I threw the parachute anchor over the side to deploy it. We were drifting slowly in the wrong direction while I did so. As soon as the anchor reached the end of the eighty yards of line it was attached to, it filled with water and opened. The boat's speed went up to over 2 knots and in an even worse direction.

I stared at the screen on the GPS in disbelief and willed the numbers it was showing, and particularly the direction, to change. They didn't. I dragged the anchor back in. I was burning with a mixture of anger and fatigue.

I threw the huge parachute into the water again in a vain hope of a different answer. I waited for it to inflate beneath the water at the end of its line. I felt the anchor kick into action as the line went taut. A few moments later the figures on the GPS confirmed the old saying that the definition of insanity is doing the same thing over and over and hoping for a different result. We were still locked in the current, still on the conveyor belt going southwest.

If I hadn't been so angry, I would have wept.

Once more I began the exhausting and laborious process of dragging the parachute anchor back onto the boat, slowly coiling the lines onto the cleats on the deck, which we'd designed for them.

It felt like the lowest point of my seemingly never-ending personal struggle with the North Pacific. Chris and I had fought our way through everything that had been put in front of us for six months. Every challenge, every setback, every heartbreak we'd found a way to overcome. Now it seemed it had all been for nothing. For the want of one or maybe two miles farther east, this heartless current was going to drag us straight past the entrance to San Francisco.

I was so consumed with rage that I just wanted something or someone to take it out on. As luck would have it, Chris chose that very moment to emerge from the cabin. "How are we doing?" he asked nonchalantly, unaware of our situation.

"How are we doing?" I snapped, spoiling for a row just to vent my own frustrations. "We're fucked! That's how we're doing! The winds changed, and we're stuck in the current being dragged south." I spat out the information like a spoiled brat.

Chris looked at the reading on the GPS, then at me, and, obviously having already worked out that I was in a shitty mood, paused for a second and then with one question defused the whole situation: "Right, then, so what are we going to do?"

With that straightforward question he immediately got to the heart of the matter. I had been working myself up into a fury because I wasn't getting what I wanted, expected, or somehow thought I deserved, behaving like a spoiled toddler about to throw his teddy bear out of his crib. I was feeling sorry for myself. A simple question from Chris had drained all of the petty anger out of the situation.

Yes, I thought, what are we going to do? Then it all became simple: remove emotion from the equation and work out the options; above all, stop feeling bloody sorry for yourself. The door to San Francisco wasn't shut yet. It was closing, but there was still a glimmer of light.

The para anchor wasn't an option. It would drag us at high speed past where we needed to be. We couldn't row out of the current because it was impossible to hold a course east into the wind.

We could, however, row north into the flow of the water streaming down from Alaska. We wouldn't make any progress, but it would slow down our drift to the south. The easterly wind was forecast to drop off and eventually veer around to the south. If we could maintain a position as far north as possible in the current until then, we might still be able to row a course into San Francisco. We agreed that it was the only option.

So once more we dug deep and took to the oars in a last effort to slow our progress south. We pointed the bow due north and did what we'd been doing for six months: we rowed relentlessly around the clock, two hours on, two hours off.

With the wind increasingly strong and from the east, it made every stint at the oars a freezing wet miserable experience, as the wind and the waves crashed directly across the boat. The rowing was heavy going. It was like rowing through the molasses of the eddies we had fought our way through months earlier.

It was the ultimate mental test. Despite the hard work we were putting in, all we managed was a slowing of our speed south from more than two knots an hour to one and a half knots an hour. Every hour we rowed we were going backward, just not as fast as we would have been if we didn't row. But we knew that difference, if we were lucky, would leave us with a way into San Francisco when the wind came around, as we dearly hoped it would.

As the sun set that day, the temperature plummeted. The rowing shifts that every day were unimaginably cold and exhausting became even tougher. The wind from the east picked up, creating a severe wind-chill factor and regularly sweeping waves across the rowing deck. Our diminishing energy levels, lack of food, and worn-out clothing made every minute on deck an agonizing trial.

At every change as I crashed into the cabin, I asked myself, "Will I be able to go back out there again?" I've no idea how, but every two hours I continued to find the will to do so. I was so wrapped up in my own fight during that time that it didn't occur to me that Chris might be having struggles of his own.

The handovers had become brief, as time in the warmth of the cabin had become increasingly precious. We barely spoke as we crossed over, each fighting his own personal battle to get through the night. With only a hot drink and a tasteless emergency biscuit at midnight to fuel our efforts, our bodies were plundering their reserves to keep us going. We were eating ourselves. By that stage neither of us had much left in the way of reserves.

A BROKEN PROMISE

BEFORE WE'D DEPARTED for Japan I'd met Chris's family. They're lovely people, enormously proud of Chris and his brother, Michael, and rightly so. The last thing his mum said to me was "Promise you'll look after Chris for me." I could see the genuine concern in her eyes when she asked it. I promised I would—"not that he'll need it."

It probably didn't appear so to Chris on occasion, but for the bulk of the voyage I believe I upheld that promise. That responsibility was one of the factors that made us such a great team. My responsibility to Chris, or rather Chris's mum, prevented me from putting our lives too far on the line.

I didn't care what happened to me in attempting to row across the Pacific. I accepted the risks. I did care what happened to Chris. The Pacific would have had to kill me to stop me if I'd rowed solo. That attitude was unthinkable with Chris on board. Chris probably saved my life just by being on the boat.

The flip side of that, and the added bonus, was that my attitude pulled Chris a little further outside his comfort zone than he might normally have chosen to go. He pulled me back, and I pulled him forward. The middle ground where we met created the rock-solid foundation of what would become an unbreakable team. We were two individuals working as one to the best of our abilities, complementing but not competing with each other. What made it all the more amazing was that we'd maintained that relationship for six months under the most arduous and challenging conditions.

That freezing night in November, battling against the frigid Alaskan current and the brutal biting wind, I forgot my promise to Mrs. Martin and stopped looking after her son. I was too busy looking after myself. Steadily, hour by hour, as we fought our greatest battle against the North Pacific, Chris began to slip into the deadly embrace of hypothermia, and I didn't see it.

Dawn broke the next day, marking the end of what was without doubt the toughest night I'd ever spent on an ocean rowing boat. It was possibly the toughest night I've ever spent anywhere. Somehow Chris and I were still managing to keep the boat's nose heading due north and the speed we were being dragged south down to less than one and a half knots.

The battle had reinvigorated me. When I had capsized, I had been totally focused on staying alive under desperate circumstances, and this last stage of the journey had given me a similar short-term vital goal to achieve. The next twenty-four hours was going to define the row, and despite the hardships, I'd grown into the challenge. When I'd discovered we were trapped in the current, I'd wanted to fight something, vent my rage, punch the North Pacific in the nose. That night's epic battle to save the whole project, as we emerged into the dawn of a new day, felt as though we might just have landed that punch.

The whole episode was a great lesson to me. It taught me that the energy surrounding any problem always comes from within. The dynamics of the problem never change, but your reaction to the problem dictates whether there's positive or negative energy surrounding it. As I'd sat on deck feeling sorry for myself, I had been consumed by negative energy, defeating myself as surely as being trapped in the current was defeating us.

Simply viewing the situation from Chris's perspective of "What are we going to do?" transformed that situation. As soon as it was obvious that there was still a way forward, however far removed from what we'd hoped, that realization brought with it a flood of positive energy. I learned many things on the North Pacific, but no lesson was as clear and profound. Defeat or victory comes from within, from a mental approach. With our approach once more positive, victory was again possible.

By 10 a.m., when Chris came out on deck to relieve me, the wind was blowing steadily from the south-southeast. I stepped into the cabin to confirm on the chart what I suspected: we'd reached our most southerly point and were now, albeit very slowly, heading north again despite still being trapped in the current. We'd turned the corner at the bottom of what would eventually resemble, on the chart, a fighter pilot's victory roll in our course toward San Francisco.

I grabbed the camera to record the momentous moment and stuck my head outside the hatch to film Chris when I told him. It was still bitter cold outside even though the sun was up, and Chris was wrapped in his eight layers of clothing with the hood of his foul-weather jacket up, the drawstring pulled as tight as possible. All I could see were his eyes staring out into oblivion.

"We've done it, mate! We're heading north again!" I shouted.

"Uh," he said, barely responsive.

My heart sank as I realized that something wasn't right. That was the best news we could have heard. Chris was an enormously positive and animated guy. It wasn't a normal reaction. It wasn't Chris at all.

"Are you okay, mate?"

Barely a grunt came back. I put the camera down and went on deck. Chris was going through the motions at the oars but hardly rowing at all. He had no strength left. He was staring past me as though he didn't know I was there.

"Fuck sake, mate. Get off the oars and get back in the cabin."

Chris stopped and slowly made his way to the hatch on all fours. I was horrified and ashamed of myself for not spotting what was happening to him earlier. His body was slowly shutting down, trying to conserve heat. One of the first signs of hypothermia is lethargy and loss of personality. The guy on the boat that morning bore almost no similarities to the Chris I knew. Another two hours in those conditions, and I've no doubt he would have collapsed. I was beside myself that I'd allowed him to get into that situation without my noticing.

"Mate, you should have said something." I said lamely.

As he crawled through the hatch, he looked back at me, trying to force a smile. "I did, mate. I told you I couldn't do that again."

I got him out of his wet clothes and into a warm sleeping bag and made some food and a hot drink with what remained of our rations. Almost immediately there was improvement, so I relaxed a little.

"Okay, mate. You get your head down now, and see how you feel in a couple of hours. You're not rowing, but come on deck and make a hot wet for us both."

Although still exhausted, he seemed a little more like the old Chris.

I went back on the oars and waited anxiously to see what the next two hours would bring. Chris came out on time, still sluggish and tired but certainly a lot better than when he'd last been rowing. "I don't want a wet, but I'll make you one," he murmured.

"No, mate, you'll make a wet for both of us. You need a warm drink inside of you."

Reluctantly he agreed, and I stopped rowing to share a drink with him. He was on the mend but a long way from being himself. He moved to take over the rowing.

"No, mate, get your head down. Come out every two hours to make sure I'm okay and make a wet, and we'll swap over later."

We carried on with that routine for the rest of the day. We were still in the current, but with the wind now coming from the south it meant that if we kept rowing we would make ground north. To make up all the ground we'd lost south, one of us had to be at the oars the whole time. There was no way that could be Chris for the time being, so I stayed on the oars.

By the evening, Chris was very much back to himself. During the day he'd come out every two hours as I'd insisted and made a drink for us both. It was usually a shared tea bag, as even our precious tea supply was now getting low. It was a massive relief to see his steady improvement during the day.

"I can row now," he said as the evening drew in.

"No, mate, I'll keep going. It's going to be freezing cold again soon, and we don't want to undo all our good work. Just keep making me wets every couple of hours."

He was adamant that he was okay to row. I was adamant that he wasn't. Less than ten hours earlier he'd been close to collapse. Another night in freezing temperatures would have put him right back to square one, or worse. He'd already rowed one more night than he'd thought he could. I wasn't going to ask him to do that again.

I rowed through the night, with Chris joining me every two hours to make a drink and argue with me about taking over. I'd decided he wasn't going to be taking over from me. I wasn't having the same issues with the cold that he was having, and besides, I owed him. While he'd rowed himself to the point of unconsciousness on my behalf, I had been blind to his worsening situation. I'd forgotten my promise to his mum. I was ashamed for having been oblivious to his worsening condition and wanted to make sure I didn't forget that promise again.

At dawn the next day the wind had come fully round to the southwest. We'd rowed almost a complete loop. Although we were still in the current, the wind was gently pushing us northeast and eventually out of its frigid grip. With our course heading exactly where we needed to go with me rowing or not, I decided to call it a day.

I crawled into the cabin next to Chris and collapsed into a deep, exhausted sleep. Not for the first time on our voyage, disaster had been avoided by the skin of our teeth. We were back on course to the Golden Gate Bridge.

BIG MACS!

WHEN I WOKE UP, Chris was back on the rowing position. He was smiling and cracking jokes, once again the bloke I knew. It was a massive relief. The sun was shining. We'd finally left the Alaskan current behind us, and the US coast was only 150 miles away.

We still had one major problem, though: we were almost completely out of food.

I rang Mos. The weather forecast made it look as if we could potentially get in within four or five days if we were lucky. We might get to port in four or five days, but we could just as easily be out here another two weeks. With Chris vulnerable to hypothermia, resupply was a must. We needed to get food on board

Any possible doubts about that necessity were removed when we used the last teabag.

"Sod that. No food is one thing, but no tea? There are limits. Let's arrange the resupply!" I said to Chris.

Mos told us that with the help of Bill Wolbach, our American film producer friend from 2001, he'd located a helicopter pilot, who was prepared to fly out and drop some food and, crucially, tea bags. We'd have to be no more than a hundred miles from the coast, though, for him to be able to safely reach us and get back. That looked like a day's or possibly two days' rowing at that point.

"Great stuff. Go for it, mate."

In the end it took three days to get close enough to California for the pilot to be able to reach us safely, the last two of which we had effectively no food. One Cup-a-Soup between us was the total ration for one of the days. The other day we had a bonus thanks to Chris's tenacity. He unpacked the front locker and contorted himself enough to jam his arm into an almost inaccessible bow locker at the front of the boat, where the original rations had been stowed.

"There's something in there, Mick, I'm certain," he assured me.

I was equally certain there wasn't but let him get on with it. When he emerged, battered and bruised, covered in scrapes and red marks, he was proudly holding an original lunch meal pack. I saluted him. There was hot chocolate, a main meal, and a dessert, all in one sealed pack. There were more calories than we'd seen in a week. It felt like a Christmas feast to us both.

Our resupply finally arrived on November 8. As we approached a hundred miles from the coast, a crazy American pilot and Vietnam War veteran named Wayne Lackey flew out in a helicopter with his copilot and friend, Gary Wooton, and a local filmmaker, Sandra Cannon.

Wayne had parked a fuel truck on a cliff road, then filled up and flown his single-engine Jet Ranger helicopter to the limit of its range to reach us. He'd estimated ten minutes over our location, leaving him with twenty minutes' fuel reserve in his tank to get back. They ended up over us for twice as long as anticipated getting the supplies down. When they flew back, Wayne later told me, his fuel indicator was showing "E" for empty as they approached the cliff. By the time they landed to refuel, he had less than ten minutes of flight time left. "That fuel truck sure was a beautiful sight, Mick!"

Wayne and his crew were exactly the sort of guys you would want to have flying your support in a war.

We were feeling the effects of a massive storm hundreds of miles to the north of us as there was a huge ocean swell. When the chopper eventually found our location, the swell was so great that our antenna was almost hitting the bottom of the helicopter as we were lifted and dropped in the huge rolling seas.

Gary lowered a black box on the end of a line, and Wayne expertly maneuvered his aircraft to drop it onto our deck. With the formidable swell and the downdraft created by the rotors, it was impossible to get it on deck. We gestured for Wayne to drop the box in the water ahead of us so we could row up to it. That would make the whole process a lot safer.

A few minutes later, we hauled the first of what would be three boxes of supplies on board. As Chris pulled the third of those treasures out of the water, he looked up to the sky and cried, "This is the best day EVER!"

We waved in gratitude to Wayne and his crew and got a thumbs-up in return from each of them. It was a fantastic moment. It was not just the relief of now having ample food to deal with all eventualities; we'd also seen other people for the first time in six months.

As Chris went to open the first of the three Styrofoam fridges, the heightened morale on board soared even further. Staring us in the face at the top of the box of supplies were two Big Macs and fries. Welcome to America! We devoured the fast food ravenously, the fact that the burgers and fries were freezing cold affecting our bliss not one iota. I doubt that anything had ever tasted quite so good to either of us.

Having demolished the Big Macs, we set about making a hot meal for the evening. It would be the first time in over three months that we could eat until full. It was a great day on board. We finally had more than enough food, and for the first time I noticed in the far distance the mountains of California. The Golden Gate Bridge was getting closer.

Though it may well have been getting closer, our arrival was no more certain then than it had been when we pushed off from Choshi in Japan. Our batteries were barely retaining any charge now, so we were trying to exist on the minimum of output. At night, we were turning our power-sapping navigation light off unless we saw any shipping close by.

The previous night, an unlit US warship had closed within yards of us before calling us on the VHF radio. "Why are you not displaying your navigation lights?" a voice demanded.

"We've just rowed from Japan, and the batteries are knackered," I answered. To which I added, rather unwisely, "Why aren't you displaying yours?"

"We're on exercise," the voice explained before disappearing into the darkness again.

The most critical thing, as usual, was the weather, in particular the wind and its direction. The forecast suggested that we might be able to make it in within four or five days, but we knew from experience that that could easily become two weeks or more.

It was constant stress, knowing that after all we'd fought through, we still might not make it in. The longer we stayed out on the ocean, the greater the chance that we would be hit by a major storm or be pushed too far south again. Despite the physical toll, the real fight was still a mental one, keeping up the belief that we could get our boat to the Golden Gate Bridge.

Two nights later it became make or break. We were within thirty miles of the coast, heading for Point Reyes. If we made it past Point Reyes close to the shore, we would be on course to row under the Golden Gate Bridge a day later. As night settled in with strong winds, it looked as though we weren't going to do that.

The wind was blowing at a steady 25 knots, with large white-capped waves rolling in front of it. The phosphorescence in the water lit up every rolling wave like a neon light show. It was good to be rowing in manageable seas, but sadly, they were going in the wrong direction. We were being pushed very slowly south of Point Reyes and San Francisco.

Heartbreakingly close to our finish, it looked as though our prize was going to be snatched away from us. Chris was on watch, so I decided to speak to our support team, who'd now arrived in San Francisco to make precautionary plans. "Mos, we're being pushed too far south, mate. We're really struggling to hold a course to make Point Reyes," I said dejectedly over the satellite phone. "We might need to think about the possibility of a tow if this carries on," I added sadly.

I'm not sure if I'd have ever accepted a tow into San Francisco, but it seemed sensible to make plans so it would at least be an option. I suspect that Chris and I would have rather rowed onto a California beach somewhere further south. That would still have felt like failure to me, but it would be preferable to an ignominious tow into port.

In the middle of the discussion I suddenly heard Chris whooping and cheering on deck. I told Mos I'd ring back and stuck my head outside. Chris was almost bouncing on his seat, shouting and hollering for joy.

"What's up, mate?" I asked.

"It's come round, mate. The bloody wind's come round!" he cried. "It's blowing us straight to Point Reyes now!"

I could feel the difference in the way the boat sat in the water. Chris was no longer fighting against the elements to hold a course. The boat was surfing down the front of the tumbling saves.

"We've cracked it!" Chris was jubilant. "We're going to get in!"

For the first time during the entire voyage, the wind did exactly what we needed it to do when we needed it to do it. The change hadn't even been forecast. If it had changed direction a couple of hours later, it would have been too late and we'd have been too far south. But it had come at precisely the right time. It felt to both of us as though the Pacific had finally said, "You know what, you blokes deserve a shot at this. You've earned it. Here's your chance, go see if you can row your boat under the Golden Gate Bridge."

It was as near to a spiritual moment as either of us would probably ever admit to experiencing. Well, that and the Big Macs.

THE FINAL PUSH

IT WAS STILL by no means a given that we'd make it into San Francisco Bay. Rowing toward an unknown point at night in strong winds with big seas is the stuff of nightmares from a skipper's point of view. But it was the chance we'd been hoping and praying for, and we were going to take it.

What followed was one of the most exhilarating and thrilling nights of the whole voyage. We were racing in front of great luminous waves with their white crests glowing in the night. We were still freezing as the biting wind tore through what was left of our protective clothing, but we were both elated at the prospect of finally achieving our goal. The Golden Gate Bridge was thirty miles along the coast once we passed Point Reyes, one day's row along a relatively protected coast away. We were going to bloody well make it. After more than six months at sea, for the first time both of us really thought we were going to do it.

When dawn broke on the crisp, clear morning of November 12, we were still running ahead of those same large waves. The only difference was that we were looking at the southern side of Point Reyes. We'd made it past the formidable point in the night. We'd managed to stay close enough to tuck into the coastline as well. Thirty of the easiest—but most nerve-wracking—miles now lay between our goal and us.

A small crab-fishing boat motored over to us as I stood in front of the cabin hatch and Chris rowed. The waves and the swell were still high, so as he came alongside there was a fifteen- to twenty-foot rise and fall between us. The first human being we'd spoken with face-to-face, apart from each other, in more than six months slid down his cabin window and looked at us, puzzled.

"You guys okay?' he shouted.

"Yep!" I answered, and we both put our thumbs up in the British tradition to emphasize the point.

He shoved the window up, drove around to the other side of our boat, and then pulled the other window down.

"Where you from?" he shouted.

"Japan!" I shouted back.

He shoved his window back up and drove off without saying a word.

"He doesn't believe us, Chris," I said, and both of us laughed out loud. I suppose it did sound a bit far-fetched.

For the rest of that glorious day, we rowed in increasingly friendlier seas. With almost all of the pressure we'd been under for the whole of the voyage now magically lifted, it was a wonderful day.

For the first time in over half a year we saw land and brilliant colors—green trees, houses, cars—other than those of the ocean. The radio picked up the local easy listening stations, and we rowed, appropriately, listening to the classic songs of the Beach Boys and the Eagles as we counted down the last few miles to our finish line.

The food we'd taken on board had turned out not to be essential in terms of fueling extra time at sea, but it had given us the energy to enjoy those last days aboard our tiny floating home. In particular, it had enabled us to savor and enjoy what we hoped would be our last twenty-four hours on board.

Normally at the end of an ocean row, the boats come straight into port from the ocean. The families of the racers embrace them and then absorb them back into their previous lives. What that means is that the team that was created on board no longer exists. People seldom have a chance to reflect on that aspect of such a grueling endeavor and appreciate it fully.

I felt that our last day's row along the coast with the threat of failure lifted and our goal within our grasp gave Chris and me a chance to savor what we'd achieved, what we'd come through together. The only reason we were in that position was that we'd forged a relationship that had created a formidable and unbreakable team.

My brother once said that rowing across an ocean is like Royal Marines training: "It just asks you how much you want to do it. If you don't want to do it, it'll find out."

The North Pacific had never stopped asking Chris and me how much we wanted to do it, with challenge after challenge. It had always reveived the same answer: "Enough to keep going!"

I'd been the first to spot the California mountain ranges, so it was only right that Chris should be the first to see the Golden Gate Bridge. It was at 5:40 a.m. on Friday the thirteenth of November. We hoped the unfortunate date would not portend any last-minute disaster.

As dawn broke with both of us on deck, we had the privilege of witnessing the most amazing sunrise, creating a spectacular silhouette of the bridge. It felt like a welcome celebration just for us.

As we slowly covered the last few miles, a flotilla of small boats came to join us. There were powerboats, sailboats, even rowing boats and a paddle boarder. Most of those on board threw cans of beer at us, they'd obviously got word of our reputations, a few actually managing to hit the target. Bill Wolbach, who'd helped sort out the resupply, even turned up to hand over my dad's old soccer shirt to me.

It had been a gift Dad had given Bill when the American had

visited our family pub. Bill had insisted that he would take it only on loan and hand it back as soon as I rowed beneath the Golden Gate Bridge. He'd flown up from Mexico to do just that.

When we'd spoken to Wayne about the supplies we needed, I'd also mentioned that we'd like a US courtesy flag to display when we rowed in, a courtesy flag being a small local flag to raise in acknowledgment to the country whose waters you're entering. The flag Wayne provided wouldn't have looked out of place flying as the ensign on a battleship. It was enormous. Chris tied it to our VHF antenna.

"Mate, we'd better see if we can grab a Union Jack off someone as well before we go under the bridge," I said to Chris.

Right on cue, a motorboat from the Golden Gate Yacht Club turned up, fully decked out with all manner of rowing club banners and Union Jack flags. We could see Chris's family and my old friend Neil Kent on board.

My mum was on board, too. It was a bittersweet moment for both of us. It was the first time we'd seen each other since my dad had died. Dad had already been gone four months, and I'd not been able to so much as hug my mum. I could see the relief in her face, but her smile was strained. The reality of Dad's loss swept over me once more. He'd have loved that day.

The boat came over and threw a British flag across to Chris. He hurriedly tied it onto the antenna on the other side of the cabin so it flew alongside the Stars and Stripes. Then we both sat down to finish the row: the first and still the only row across the North Pacific from Japan to the Golden Gate Bridge.

I get asked a lot how it felt after all those years and all those setbacks, finally arriving beneath that bridge. We had our back to the bridge, so I felt it before I saw it. As the shadow of the bridge fell over us, I felt the drop in temperature. It was almost like a cool embrace. Then, a minute or two later, we could see the span of the bridge. Finally, it was the moment I'd dreamed about for so many years, looking straight up and seeing the Golden Gate Bridge directly above me. I'm not sure that words, certainly not mine, can explain how that felt.

A gun was fired into the air at 8:35 a.m., as we crossed directly under the center point of the bridge. We'd done it. We'd just completed the Everest of ocean rowing, one of the world's last great firsts.

I reached forward to Chris, and we clasped hands. Neither of us can remember what was said. I suspect there was some cheering and "Well done"s. It's all a bit of a blur. What was most important was that we'd completed what we set out to do.

The Golden Gate Yacht Club, soon to become the proud custodians of the America's Cup, had kindly offered to host us. As we rowed alongside the pontoon it seemed as though most of the population of San Francisco had come to greet us. The floating docks were so full of people that they were almost underwater.

An enormous cheer went up as we threw our lines ashore, and I saw in the crowd on the dock among the spectators a guy who looked like he'd just stepped off a movie set. He was tall, had film-star good looks, sported a sharp suit, and was engulfed by the press. Chris jumped off and fell into the arms of his girlfriend, Sandra, and his waiting family. I was looking for my mum. As I stepped off the boat, the film-star guy said, "Congratulations," shook my hand, and remarked on the condition of my bare feet.

"I'm off straight from here to the auditions for *The Hobbit*," I said, laughing. My feet did look unusually flat and hairy.

Then I said, "Excuse me, mate" and started to step around him. "I've got to get to my mum."

At which point Mayor Gavin Newsom of San Francisco, as I'd later find out he was, gallantly made a path for me through the crowd to reach my mum, who was standing at the back. I reached out, took her in my arms, hugged her, told her I loved her, and apologized for how bad I smelled. She didn't seem to mind.

EPILOGUE

AS FABULOUS and wonderfully hospitable as the welcome in San Francisco was for us, it came with mixed emotions for me. It was the first time I'd seen Mum since we'd lost Dad; if his loss didn't dominate the atmosphere, the fact that he wasn't able to enjoy our success with us did. He would have loved it.

My wife wasn't there to share the experience with me, either. Grace was still in the United Kingdom. As I rowed under the Golden Gate Bridge, she was at home packing to depart for Heathrow airport that day. The intransigence of the immigration systems in both the United Kingdom and Nigeria meant that it would be another three months until we saw each other again. If there was one person who would have loved and appreciated that day as much as my dad, it was Grace.

After I stepped ashore, I found that Amanda from our "pop-up" voluntary support team had thoughtfully set up a Skype link, which would let me speak to and see Grace on a computer screen at least. I didn't even know what Skype was at the time. It was a lovely thought but it was a moment we should have shared in person that circumstances stole from us. It was the low point of an otherwise jubilant day.

I'd always known that San Francisco would be the greatest city in the world to row into from the North Pacific, and so it proved to be. It's perhaps arrogant to wish for more when you've just been given a prize as enormous as that. But I do wish I could have shared that day with two more of the people I loved.

There was one massive high point about reaching San Francisco: this time, I'd brought the film back. It had been a very different story from my solo trip, but no less remarkable. I had done what I'd promised myself I would do: I'd gone back and gotten the story again, and now we could tell it.

Two years later, Discovery Channel would broadcast the documentary *Rowing the Pacific*. It wouldn't get any better than that until I published this book, my ultimate ambition.

There are inevitably two questions whenever you step off an ocean rowing boat: "Why do it?" and "What next?" There's a third one too: "How do you go to the loo?" But you already know the answer to that.

Well, there won't be another row. I flirted with the idea a couple of times, and there's not a day that passes I don't wish I was on a rowing boat back on an ocean. But some things can't be surpassed, and rowing the North Pacific is one of them.

I always answered "Why do it?" with "Why not?" Why wouldn't you want to row across an ocean? It was as simple as that to me. In 2013, though, I discovered that there might be a little more to it than that.

That year Jackie Grenham, or "Mrs. G," as I knew her, the mother of an old friend of mine from the marines, asked me if I could organize a flight to the Falkland Islands for her son Steve's fiftieth birthday. Steve Grenham and I had been in the marines together, and we had both served in the Falkland Islands war in 1982. As veterans we were eligible to return to the islands on concessionary flights with the Ministry of Defence. Mrs. Grenham wanted Steve to return to mark his birthday and just needed some help sorting out the details. When everything was done, she said to me, "Why don't you go with him, Mick?"

It was something I'd never considered, but on reflection I thought it seemed like a good idea. "Why not? Why not go back?" So Steve and I returned to the islands together thirty-one years after fighting for its liberation.

I had barely emerged from training when the war began in 1982. Only seventeen, I found myself waiting to disembark from my troop landing ship anchored in San Carlos Water on East Falkland, or, as it would become more famously known, "Bomb Alley."

My ship was hit before I managed to disembark. Two Argentinian A-4 Skyhawks screamed in early one morning at ultralow level and dropped their bombs on the first troop ship hit in the war, my ship, the Royal Fleet Auxiliary landing ship *Sir Lancelot*. Until then the warships had taken the brunt of the attacks.

Fortunately for us, the aircraft had come in at such low level and high speed that the bombs they dropped failed to explode. That left us, after the attack, relatively unscathed but with a thousand-pound bomb lodged inside the ship ready to go off. Alarms sounded, and "Abandon ship!" blared out of the loudspeakers. When I finally stepped ashore in the Falklands, I had only the clothing I stood up in, my weapon, and not even a pair of my own boots. The efforts of the Argentine Air Force that morning had effectively ended my operational role in the war, but not my experiences there.

Days later, with the rest of my section who'd escaped from the *Sir Lancelot*, I was about to embark on her sister ship *Sir Galahad*. We'd hitched a lift to catch up with our troop headquarters. I'd passed my driving test only weeks before the conflict, so by chance I was detailed along with my friend Spot Balshaw to drive two Land

Rovers onto the ship as a favor for another unit that was moving location.

When we reached the landing craft to transport us to the ship, my section boarded, but they stopped Spot and me from driving on. "Ship's hold is full," they said. No room for any vehicles. Apparently, the Welsh Guards who'd recently arrived in the islands as reinforcements were on board with all their equipment.

On a freezing cold day with sometimes near-horizontal driving rain, we were turned back. We were the last two people refused entry onto *Sir Galahad*. We were utterly dejected.

Two days later, the ship was destroyed in another Argentinian air attack at Fitzroy. Fifty-six men were killed in total, forty-eight of them on *Sir Galahad*, with many others seriously injured and badly burned. It was the biggest single British loss of life in the war. My mate and I had missed it by sheer luck.

A few days later I had the grim honor of helping bury twenty-one of our dead in a temporary grave at Teal Inlet, a small settlement on the way to Stanley. It was the day after my eighteenth birthday and the day after the battle for Mount Longdon had begun. Eighteen of the guys lying in the temporary grave stretching out in front of us were from 2 Para (the Parachute Regiment), two of them even younger than I. Standing at attention, saluting those guys who'd fallen, while "The Last Post" played, looking down at the row of body bags in that shallow, muddy hole, is a memory from that conflict that I have never forgotten.

That fateful refusal to board the *Galahad* and the emotional mass burial showed me at an incredibly young age the random and fragile nature of fate, much more so than any of the actual combat. I'd never really recognized that though.

When Steve and I went back in 2013, it brought home to me for the first time the huge significance of that episode in my life, something I'd never really considered previously. Back in the islands, I realized that my pursuit of the first North Pacific crossing was irrevocably connected to my experiences as a young man in that war. For the first time, I came to terms with the enormous impact of those experiences and their effects. I must say, despite the tragic nature of all conflicts, I considered the impact to be largely positive. As regrettable and avoidable as any war is, if it had to happen, I was glad to have been part of it. I came back a better person. I'd departed for the Falklands secure in the immortality of youth and returned acutely aware of the luck that governs all of our fates. I came back grateful for life, with a huge appetite for it and acutely aware of its fleeting nature. I'd also learned, as anyone who's been in a conflict will tell you, that colors are never brighter than when you think you may be looking at them for the last time. There's an addiction to that kind of intensity of life and the quest to complete one of the world's last great firsts, rowing the North Pacific from Japan to San Francisco, would be my way of dealing with that addiction.

Combined with that enhanced appetite for life, I felt a huge debt to those who hadn't come back, guys who'd done much more than I to deserve the incredible heroes' welcome we all received when we returned home. Guys, some of whom I'd helped bury and left behind. Repayment of that debt for me—again, not that I knew it at the time—became part of the reason to row the North Pacific. That would matter, it would have significance, and it would justify, at least in my own mind, coming back alive when better men than I hadn't. I hadn't wasted the extra time I'd been granted. Those were the driving reasons why I'd wanted to row across an ocean; I had simply not been aware of them until returning with Steve to the Falkland Islands.

Steve had served with 42 Commando in 1982 as an eighteen-year-old marine. When we returned in 2013, we revisited all the sites that had significance for the pair of us. Mount Harriet was the most important for Steve. He'd fought his way up that mountain overlooking

Port Stanley with the rest of his unit at night in the last days before the Argentine surrender on June 14.

At the very top of Harriet, he told me that he'd been having increasing problems over the years coming to terms with some of his experiences in the war. It had begun to negatively impact his life more and more, until his wife and family, in particular his brother Tony, had begged him to look for help.

Finally, he had gone to one of the largest charities in the United Kingdom looking after the welfare of British service personnel and asked for that help. They told him he ticked all the boxes for post-traumatic stress disorder (PTSD) except one—suicide—and advised that he go away for three months, no drugs or alcohol, come back, and then he could be diagnosed officially.

Standing on the top of Mount Harriet, next to the cross that's mounted there as a memorial to the guys that died on that mountain, Steve turned to me and said, "If I could do that, Mick, I wouldn't need their help, would I?"

I was horrified that he'd gotten that response, not least because I knew he'd never ask for help again once he'd had the door closed in his face.

"I'll tell you what, mate," I said, "let's work on a project that'll get you through three months without booze or drugs."

Looking down at the coastline of the Falklands surrounding us, I said, "Let's kayak around the Falkland Islands. How hard can that be?" (Very, as it turned out.) The story of how we tried to do that would eventually become the answer to the question "What next?"

That simple idea would evolve into a series of kayak expeditions and races over two years, stretching from Westminster Bridge to Loch Ness and out to the Yukon, before Steve and I finally returned to the Falklands to make good on our promise early in 2017 with a nine-day expedition kayaking around the principal battle sites of the Falklands War. It helped Steve, and it allowed me to continue repaying my debt. It's a debt I hope to continue to be able to repay with the project we set up to achieve this. The Cockleshell Endeavour, www.cockleshellendeavour.com, is now ongoing, providing veterans and serving personnel alike a way to use adventure training as a means to help in their recovery from injury or PTSD. In conjunction with the Royal Marines Kayaking Association, the project will continue to raise awareness of the issues of PTSD and funding for the Royal Marines Charity. I can't think of a more fitting legacy to my rowing adventures.

When Chris and I arrived in San Francisco after the successful North Pacific crossing in 2009, my old friend from marine training Ross Cluett, who had run the last 15 miles of that eventful 30-miler with me, sent an email. Ross had also been part of my section that had walked onto the *Galahad* when I was turned away, all of whom survived.

The email was a simple message with a big meaning: "Great effort, Royal."

"Royal" is the informal name for a brother Royal Marine.

Ross served his full time out in the Corps before leaving as a sergeant major at the top of his branch. I had a huge amount of respect for Ross, and it meant a lot to me to receive that message of congratulations from him.

I replied, thanking him, and said, "Amazing isn't it mate? My finest effort as a Royal Marine comes eighteen years after I left."

It seems that there may well be some truth in the old saying "Once a marine, always a marine."

ACKNOWLEDGMENTS

THERE ARE SO MANY PEOPLE TO THANK for making this book and the story contained in it happen; the danger is forgetting someone. Hopefully that won't be the case, but here goes nothing!

Thanks foremost to my family—my parents in particular—for demonstrating how to truly enjoy life and set wildly unachievable goals . . . and then achieve them.

Thanks to my beautiful wife, Grace, who joined this ocean rowing circus in full flow and put up with it, and who continues to put up with me. No Nigerian woman has ever rowed across an ocean yet, Grace . . . just saying.

To my brother, Steve, thank you for being the best example to grow up with, for your perceptive taste in music, and for setting the bar for ocean rowing partners.

Thanks to the wider Dawson and Gray families for helping to provide a warm, secure, colorful, fun childhood that allowed me to dream big. Thanks to the ones who are sadly no longer with us but are much missed, as well as to those of you who are still kicking around causing mischief. I couldn't have grown up with better people around me.

Thanks to Andy Smith for "retraining" as a maritime electrical engineer just so you could keep our conveyor belt of rowing adventures on track. It's hard to believe we've been mates for more than forty-three years now. You must be really old!

To Paul Orchard-Lisle, thank you for your constant support in my aims to successfully navigate across the Atlantic and North

Pacific Oceans, despite my having frequently demonstrated an inability to navigate successfully across central London.

To Bill and Luke Wolbach at Lantern Films in the United States, thanks for being great mates and constant sources of support and encouragement over many years and even more pints of Guinness.

To Ellen and Bob and all the guys at the Golden Gate Yacht Club, thank you for creating such a great welcome.

Thanks to Mos Morris for showing me the things I still needed to know to successfully cross the North Pacific while also confirming my belief that Speedo bathing trunks should be illegal.

Special thanks to Chris Martin for putting up with me for six and a half months on a rowing boat. I told you it would be fun.

Thanks to Des Hawking and his team for building the perfect rowing boat.

Thanks to Lee Bruce at OceanMet for such sterling, if sometimes a little scary, weather support.

Thanks to Michael Kobold of Kobold Watches for providing me with such a great time piece.

To the guys down in Poole when we were finishing the build on *Bo* who helped find solutions for all our last-minute problems. To Pip Riley, a good mate and top bloke who came up with our steering system solution, and to Mick and Steve at Hypro Marine in Lymington (brothers, appropriately enough), who built it.

To Andy Rice, who owns Elite Fabrication & Welding, thank you for solving all our stainless-steel issues, often personally and invariably with little or no notice. A good "wet" of tea at your place, too, mate.

To Pete Jones, that rarest of creatures—a trustworthy yacht broker—for introducing me to many of those people. Your shout for coffee, I believe.

To Femi Otedola, my old boss in Nigeria; without your sponsorship of the project in 2009, we would not have reached Japan, let alone the Golden Gate Bridge. Thank you.

To the countless people in Boston who supported and followed all the rowing projects right from day 1. I really can't list all of them, but your efforts were and are greatly appreciated.

Thanks to the Boston Council, Duncan Browne at the *Boston Standard*, and local BBC Radio, which have and continue to support and champion an "old-boys" effort over the years.

To Simon Chalk, thank you for giving me the chance to build a new state-of-the-art rowing boat after I mislaid my own and for giving me the opportunity to be involved in the 2005 ocean rowing race.

To Maurice and Ann Stevens for their constant encouragement, support, and friendship since my time at Brighton Film School. And, of course, to Brighton Film School and its creator and then owner, Franz von Habsburg.

To the Cowbridge House Inn (the only pub in England with that name) in Boston. My family's pub. To all the people who worked there, socialized there, and came together to support all the rowing projects over the years, thank you.

Most important, I'd like to thank Wendy Keller, my literary agent. Without her expertise and belief in this book, it would never have been published. Thank you for believing in the story and finding such a fantastic platform to tell it from. I am in your debt.

To Phil Revzin, with whom I worked over the last ten months editing and creating the story enclosed within these covers; your help, encouragement, and suggestions were invaluable.

And a huge thanks, of course, to my publisher Hachette Book Group for having faith in the story and giving me the chance to tell it on a global scale, particularly my editor, Kate Hartson, and her assistant, Grace Johnson.

Many other friends, supporters, and sponsors have helped over the years—too many to list—so if I've failed to thank you personally, I hope you see expressed in the story my gratitude to all those who have helped make my adventures and this book a reality.

Big thanks to all my friends in Japan, the members at Choshi Yacht Club in particular. Especially my friend Kaz—I'd still be stuck in customs without your help.

My sponsors in Japan, Cushman & Wakefield. Thank you for your constant support over the years, in particular; Bill Krueger, Stefan Hall, and Fumie Kitamura. Karaoke anyone?

And thanks, of course, for the consistent help and support from the Japanese Coast Guard.

My most sincere thanks go to the people who made sure this story had the chance of a happy ending: the Falmouth Coastguard in the United Kingdom; the servicemen and -women of the US Coast Guard in Kodiak, Alaska: Commander Beverly Carter, Patrick Walker, and the aircrew that flew to my rescue. I'll be over to buy you that beer as soon as possible, Patrick. Thanks also to Captain Peter Winter, the master of the *Hanjin Philadelphia*, and his fantastic crew. Without your skill and professionalism, I would not be here now. I owe you my life.

And to our 2009 Pacific saviors, my crazy friend Wayne Lackey, who courageously flew out the best-tasting McDonald's in history in our moment of need, along with his equally crazy copilot, Gary Wooton, and the lovely Sandra Cannon. We really enjoyed the wine-tasting tour when we got in, too!

Last but by no means least, I would like to pay tribute to an old and much-missed friend who was part of all my ocean rowing adventures and whom I'd known most of my life: Neil Kent, who was killed while pursuing his passion on the Isle of Man preparing for the Manx Grand Prix motorcycle race, which he'd won the previous year, in 2011.

I dedicated this book to Mum and Dad, Neil. Which I know you'd have approved of, but it's in memory of you. Raise a glass with my Dad for me, mate.

ABOUT THE AUTHOR

MICK DAWSON was born in Boston, Lincolnshire, on the east coast of England in 1964. After leaving school in 1980, he joined the Royal Marines, in which he served for eleven years before moving on to a career as a professional sailor skippering private yachts around the globe. Looking for a challenge in 2001, he rowed across the Atlantic Ocean together with his brother, Steve. In the eight years that followed, Mick became one of the most experienced and successful ocean rowers in the world, completing a second transatlantic row and attempting two solo rows across the North Pacific Ocean. Finally, in 2009, along with his friend and rowing partner Chris Martin, he successfully rowed across the North Pacific from Choshi, Japan, to the Golden Gate Bridge in San Francisco, a voyage of nearly six and a half months of rowing and a total of almost 7,000 miles. He and Chris hold a Guinness World Record as the first team to row the Pacific Ocean from west to east. It is one of the last great firsts.

Mick now lives in East Sussex with his wife, Grace. His new project, The Cockleshell Endeavour, www.cockleshellendeavour. com, in conjunction with the Royal Marines Kayaking Association, is designed to assist former and serving service personnel who are struggling with post-traumatic stress disorder or physical injuries. The project also raises money for the Royal Marines Charity, www. theroyalmarinescharity.org.uk.

Mick is a filmmaker, motivational speaker, and author. He still sails professionally and doesn't rule out further adventures.

www.189days.com